Chablis

BERNARD GINESTET'S GUIDE
TO THE VINEYARDS OF FRANCE

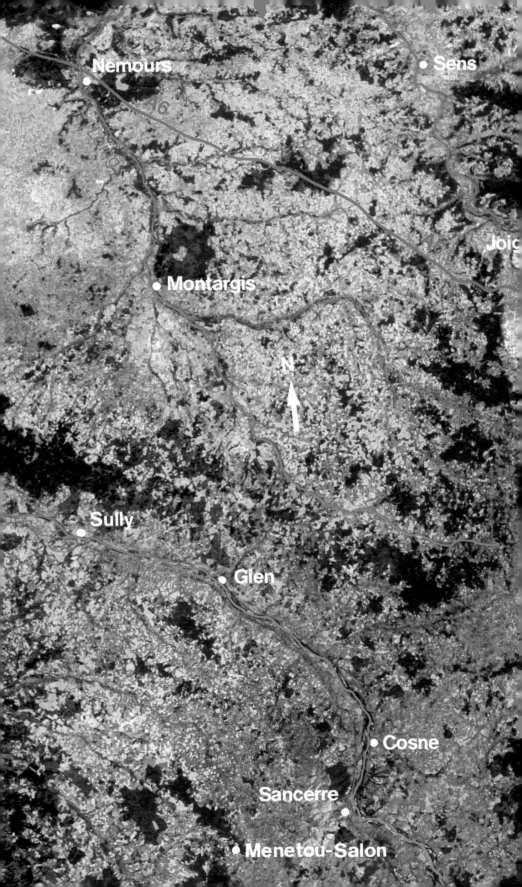

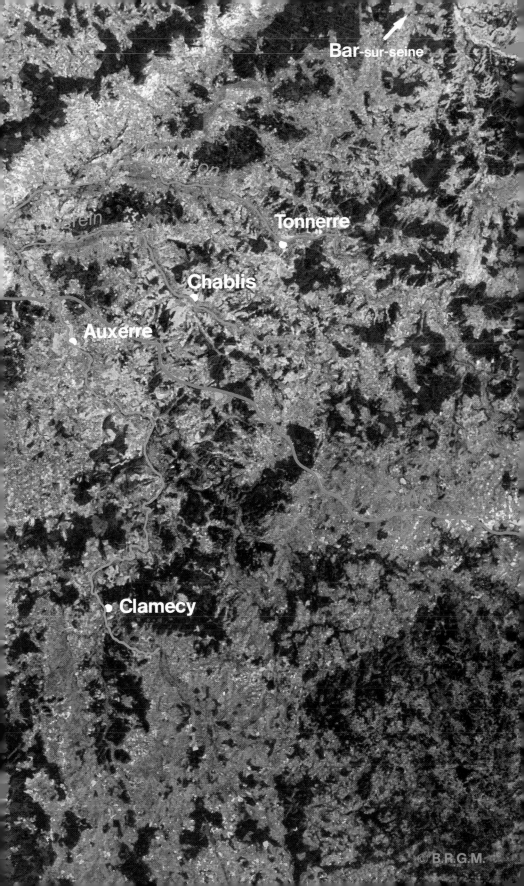

Bar-sur-seine

Tonnerre

Chablis

Auxerre

Clamecy

© B.R.G.M.

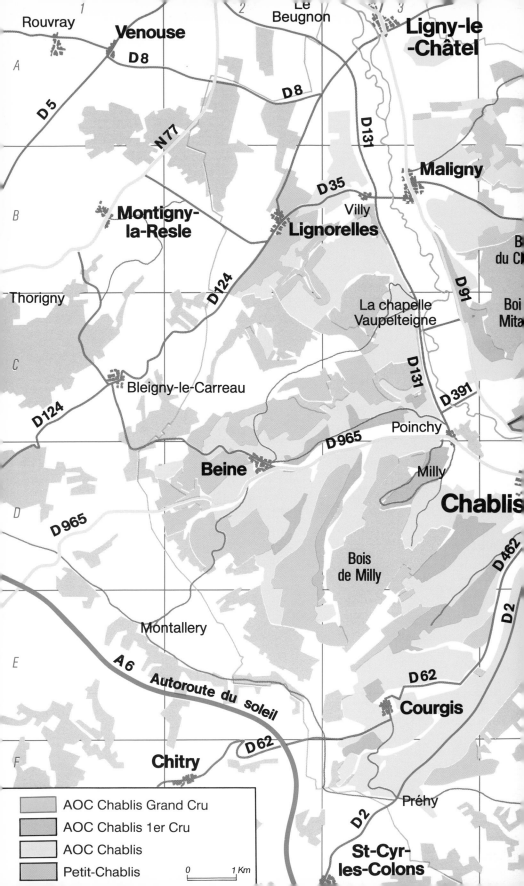

Rouvray

Venouse

D 8

D 5

Le Beugnon

Ligny-le -Châtel

D 8

N 77

D 131

Maligny

D 35

Villy

Montigny- la-Resle

Lignorelles

Thorigny

D 124

La chapelle Vaupelteigne

D 91

Boi du Cl

Boi Mita

Bleigny-le-Carreau

D 124

D 131

D 391

Poinchy

D 965

Milly

Beine

Chablis

D 965

Bois de Milly

D 462

D 2

Montallery

A 6

Autoroute du soleil

D 62

Courgis

Chitry

D 62

D 2

Préhy

St-Cyr- les-Colons

AOC Chablis Grand Cru

AOC Chablis 1er Cru

AOC Chablis

Petit-Chablis

0   1 Km

Bernard Ginestet

Foreword by Nicholas Faith

Chablis

Translated by John L. Meredith

BERNARD GINESTET'S GUIDE
TO THE VINEYARDS OF FRANCE

Jacques Legrand

Originated and produced by:

Jacques Legrand SA

English version edited by:

Editor:	Nicholas Faith
Assistant editor:	Tamara Thorgevsky
Translator:	John L. Meredith
Copy editor:	Barbara Mellor
Editorial secretary:	Christine Fourton
Art director:	Henri Marganne
Layout:	Claire Forgeot

ISBN 0-582-07543-2 for Longman UK distribution
ISBN 2-905969-34-2 for the rest of the world

Printed in Belgium by Brepols, Turnhout

Foreword

Sometimes my dear old friend Bernard Ginestet does 'carry on alarming', as my old nanny used to say. This volume shows him at his most characteristic: his whimsicality sometimes defies translation, but neither it nor his deviations from the strict path of duty can hide his generosity of spirit, or his profound knowledge of the history, folklore, wine and wine-making of Chablis, a mastery which is the more impressive because he is not a native of the region.

At his best – which is most of the time – as in his account of how the geologists, casually and unwittingly, set off the Great Kimmeridgian War, he shows himself a real master of viti-farce, a much neglected theatrical form. He has also performed a useful task in collecting many of the local folk-poems, which John Meredith has miraculously managed to translate into an entirely appropriate English poetic form and language in a real technical and poetic tour de force.

The war was a prime example of the way the locals, helped by the whims of modern geologists, have managed to complicate what should have been one of the simplest of all great French vineyards. There has never been any real disagreement about the fundamentals: Chablis is a great white wine made solely from the chardonnay grape from a small area of Kimmeridgian chalk on the banks of the aptly-named River Serein, a hundred and fifty miles south-east of Paris. The wine, crisp, flavoursome, elegant, was clearly destined by nature to enhance the flavour of all manner of fish, most obviously oysters and other crustaceans. And that's that. The only apparent problem was to guard against the late frosts inevitable in such a northerly vineyard, a problem easily overcome with low-technology smudge-pots or water spraying.

Moreover the local community has always been close: it formed one of the first major wine-making cooperatives in the country in the early 1920s, and since then 'La Chablisienne', unlike many of its equivalents in the rest of France, has set rigorous standards of quality which ensure that 'real' Chablis can easily be distinguished from the numerous imitators which are at one and the same time an irritant and a tribute to the quality of the original. Equally the local merchants, unlike their fellows in the Gironde, have not been foreigners, have not spent the past centuries grinding the faces of the poor growers. They have made their own contribution to the region's renown.

Nevertheless the locals did make heavy weather of the crucial problem of defining (and possibly enlarging) the vineyard's qualitative divisions, an argument complicated by the geologists. Fortunately even Bernard (no great lover of all French official decisions as can be seen in his volume on Saint-Emilion) cannot find serious fault with the outcome. Which leaves us to discuss and enjoy the wine – and resolve the one unresolved (and, happily, unresolvable) point of disagreement – should Chablis have anything to do with oak? For myself, I think not: I'm sick and tired of chardonnays devoured by wood. But I think we should certainly open a bottle or two to make sure.

Nicholas Faith

Contents

Naturally yours... Chablis

*For Raymond Dumay
and Pierre Poupon,
Masters of Burgundy,
with affection*

"Dry, limpid, perfumed, lively and light."

My friend Raymond Dumay, the writer from Burgundy, has just put his glass of Chablis down on the table. He has not clicked his tongue, as romantic custom would have it, but his verbal sketch is evocative, the more so as it is enhanced by the hint of a country accent as rough as the rocky hillsides of Vaudésir. When Raymond Dumay says "parrrfumé", the very word has an inimitable and subtle bouquet, like the wine of Chablis. Chablis! A name that rolls off the tongue and to the ear. A delicate, unassuming word, it makes hardly any noise and yet asserts its presence, filling the silence without piercing it. If anybody offers me Chablis, I pause to relish the music of its name before allowing myself to be captivated by what it lies in the glass. The English are not the only foreigners to be ensnared by its charms. For them, Chablis means "a great, dry white wine". And it must be confessed that "Chablis" is easier and more agreeable to say. So then, we can understand the popularity of this name throughout the world. And, thanks to Chablis, there is hardly a foreigner today who does not know at least one word of French. If they use it haphazardly

---

◄ *The cellar of the Obédiencerie bears witness to the ancient wine-producing tradition of the region.*

A typical Chablis landscape at Les Vaillons, with vines rising up the slopes. ▶

when speaking of other wines that is the penalty to be paid for world renown. Eau-de-Cologne has long since made money for cities other than Cologne! And so Chablis has prospered. But apart from the ringing magic of its name, it had to have the quality needed to become world famous in the first place.

As we shall see, this goes back to the time of the Flood, with the formation of deposits known as Kimmeridgian clay. Now our task consists in distinguishing good from inferior wine, and, of course, the genuine article from misnamed California chardonnay.

Chablis is an *appellation d'origine*. Moreover, it is declined like the *mensa* of school Latin lessons: Chablis *Grand Cru*, Chablis *Premier Cru*, Chablis *(stricto sensu)* and Petit-Chablis. Each comes from a registered area, with an original source. From the greatest to the smallest, there is a system. Yes, one does exist, although it is not always clear. If Chablis can be distinguished by its clarity in the glass, this is not always the case on the ground. For nearly a century, it appears that the men of Chablis have been seeking their true identity, sometimes disputing among themselves as to each man's right to his title. But for some time now things have become more serene on either side of the Serein, a tributary of the Yonne which flows across the appellation, just as the Seine bisects Paris and the Mediterranean formerly used to cross France. This book appears just at the right time to record that the men of peace have accomplished their mission. For the first time, in a period when we are for ever striving for more precision in our knowledge, it has been possible to draw up a collection of finely detailed maps of the Chablis vineyards. This is not just a token gesture: their publication will be valuable not only to the professionals of the region (and a host of others!) but will also serve as a guide to all lovers of good wine, for whom every reference on a label should represent a reality.

Chablis is an *appellation d'origine*. A wine's origins may be viewed as a sort of etymology : its derivation and its explanation. At Chablis, or more exactly in the Chablis area, this term assumes a particular depth of meaning owing to all that it implies. The *terroir*, that is, the geological nature of the terrain, the subsoil, the climate and microclimates, the hill slopes and their exposure to the sun are essential factors. "And man?" you may ask, "and the vines?" Indeed, I do not underestimate their significance, but above all else, I would like to acknowledge the essential role played by natural factors and conditions. Without them, the same people and the same vines would not have been able to achieve this kind of *chef-d'œuvre*.

If we are to believe the legend of Chablis as told by Odette Magarian, the inventor of pruning was a donkey which, feeling in need of a snack one afternoon, browsed on the leaves of a vine. I find that this legend does less than justice to the romance of Chablis and I tend to prefer the story that Peau d'Ane (the bewitched donkey of a French fairy-tale), having finally shed her skin to become the marvellous Mélusine thanks to the Queen of the Frogs, created the golden chardonnay grape with a wave of her magic vine-twig, all because a family of goldfinches (*chardonnerets*) had nowhere to nest. Without wishing to rewrite history, we can always dream up another legend, and we should heed the poet Patrice de La Tour du Pin when he says that "any country without legends will be condemned to die of cold". On this subject, the sensitivity of the Chablis vineyards to frost is legendary and is confirmed almost every May by temperatures which can drop to minus 8 °C (20 °F). In order to counteract the baleful influence of the May moon, the men of Chablis spray the vines with water, surrounding the buds with cocoons of ice, so "freezing" the interior temperature of these micro-igloos and protecting them from the extreme cold. And here legend turns up again. One very cold night at the beginning of May, Martin Simon was going back home from old mother Dondaine's bar, after spending a memorable evening with fifteen young vignerons from the Chablis area. Old mother Dondaine had just broached another barrel to accompany a "spread" just as Martin Simon liked. There was broth with salt pork and peas, followed by whitebait caught in a bow-net the evening before near the mill known as Les Roches, and three splendid geese roasted on a three-pronged spit in the central fireplace: the culinary art at its finest. Madame Dondaine owed a debt of gratitude to the boys: the feast had been promised them in return for completely renovating her pantry. By tradition in Chablis, all local vignerons were also woodmen and builders. The work had been swiftly and satisfactorily concluded. In five Sundays, despite the disapproval of the priest, the pantry had been even better restored than the vestry two years previously (which had cost a fortune). And old mother Dondaine discharged her part of the bargain equally swiftly and satisfactorily. Everybody left happy after a leisurely meal (even today, the men of Chablis hold the record for prolonged dining). So, at two o'clock in the morning, Martin Simon was returning home to Fyé, his cart bumping along on the dry gravel track between La Maladière and Les Grenouilles. His horse, Plato, wondered what it was all about, being little accustomed to nocturnal expeditions. The night was bitingly cold. The moon was full, with an orange cast. The stars were shining.There was sure to be a dawn frost. Just before the hill at Bréchain, when Plato began to slow down, Martin Simon was seized with a desire to relieve himself. And it must be admitted that after all he had drunk at mother Dondaine's, he had good reason. He drew Plato to a halt (the poor beast must have been pleased, seeing before him the length of the hill he had to climb). Martin Simon emptied his bladder as copiously as he could on a superb vine. That night, all the vines on the slopes of Les Grenouilles were killed by frost. Except for one, miraculously spared: the one "watered" by Martin, which at the break of day glistened in the cold morning light with perfectly solidified festoons of topaz. Inside these crystals, the tender buds had survived. Within all living memory in Chablis, they produced the finest grapes ever. This is how Martin Simon, who does not even have a street named after him in Chablis, invented the technique of watering the vineyards against the spring frosts – by chance, under a night sky and through force of necessity.

A couple of centuries ago the climate of Chablis may well have been colder than it is today. Certainly its difficulties often cooled the ardours of the most determined growers. Although Chablis is one of the oldest growing regions

The slopes which are both the most renowned for their quality and the most exposed to frost are equipped with pipes to sprinkle the vines, so protecting them from spring frosts. ▶

of France, climatically it is particularly vulnerable. Of all the vineyards in the Parisian Basin, this is the one most threatened by frosts. The list of catastrophes is long. In years such as 1887 or 1957 everything was destroyed. At such times starting all over again from scratch required unshakeable confidence. Sometimes one area is more affected than another: Grenouilles may lose only ten per cent of its vines, whereas the lower slopes of Vaulorent may be completely devastated. When there is a clear sky and a north wind in April or May, all a grower's hopes may be swallowed up in the freezing corridor of the Serein, to perish at dawn. The Chablis chardonnays are destined all too often to be shot at dawn.

The growers developed defences to protect their vines against the excesses of the so-called temperate climate. They were aware that they made one of the best white wines in the world, but at the rate of one worthwhile harvest out of three, they could equally well have been tempted to breed sheep! From the fifties, two schools began to compete, each choosing its own weapon against the cold, like a mediaeval duel with one opponent taking the sword and the other the axe. Frost spells death: it had to be fought against. Some called on fire, for where there is fire there is heat and even smoke is a good protection; the others called on water to help them. The second choice is more efficient but more dangerous, for if it fails just once the results are fatal. Today, the great vineyards of Chablis are dependent on the skill and ability of their plumbing engineers. Near Beine, an artificial lake was created to water the hundred or so hectares of vines round about. Everything had been taken into consideration – except the catfish which eventually blocked the watering sprays! So my friends, when you sit sipping a Fourchaume in the cosy comfort of your home, spare a thought for those on duty perpetually in the meteorological station of Saint-Georges d'Auxerre. Day and night they calculate the probability of a nocturnal frost in Chablis and telephone the local growers to warn them of the dangers threatening the bottle which you will eventually open four years later. Today, the weathermen fill the role once played by soothsayers and priests, who after all could do no more than invoke the saints and encourage their parishioners to light candles.

For a long time in Chablis, the priests ruled the roost. Historically, it could be claimed that the pioneers of the vines were the clergy. The first Christians in Gaul are said to have celebrated their daring masses with the wine of Blanchot. The power of the clergy lasted until the end of the *ancien régime*, when the people decided to cut themselves off from the reigning monarchs, be they princes of the blood or of the Church. When the Revolution had not yet reached the gates of Versailles, an accusing wind was already blowing over Chablis.

More traditional than water, but more expensive to use, the "frost-stoppers" often burn domestic fuel oil to heat the air. ▶

The photos on this page show the full panoply of the "warriors against the cold".

From top to bottom and left to right: watering in Beauroy (detail), heating the vines by candles, by gas and by "brentag"; and a thermometer with a warning system in case of frost.

The court records of the 1780s bristle with incidents concerning the priest of Chablis, a certain Pierre-Joseph-Alexandre Auban, and his flock. Menu de Chomorceau, the judge, had his hands full with the endless misdemeanours of this troublesome priest and his flock. The wine of Chablis featured strongly in the story, sometimes as an element of provocation, sometimes as a soothing balm able to restore ruptured friendships – sometimes both at the same time. During divine service, the third churchwarden, the bell-ringers and other impious supernumeraries used to gulp down the priest's bottles, making an almighty din. Then the songs from the vestry drowned those of the choir.

Living at the same time as the priest Auban was Nicolas-Edme Restif, known as Rétif de La Bretonne, a prolix and muddle-headed writer who yet was sometimes inspired and who left behind him works totalling some sixty thousand pages. It was Baudelaire who asked: "Where then is Restif, from whom excellent and delightful extracts are to be taken?" He was born in Sacy, a little village to the south of Chablis, and the best of his writing depicts the condition of the peasant in the eighteenth century, in particular in *La Vie de mon père*. All the rituals which today make up the local traditions are described with the minute detail of a Brueghel. Customs and habits, fêtes, births, marriages and deaths, relationships between neighbours, work on the land, leisure and games, all are vividly described because they had been experienced by the writer at first hand. I recommend this book to anyone wishing to look further into the rural spirit and ancestral heritage of the region. We observe that the wine of Chablis presides at important ceremonies and that, for example, a proposal of marriage is sealed with cream cheese accompanied by a special "bottle of white". We also see the temperament of the people: "We have been to an elder sister's marriage, a decent girl, but a simple soul, who has married without love, without hate, and who from the very first moment after the ceremony humbly considered herself the servant of her husband, he being in turn a sturdy peasant, an excellent worker, a thrifty man, a lover of wine, yet scarcely drinking any because it is better to sell it, spending his days off not in savouring the delights of love, but in going over his accounts, checking his fields of vines, and reflecting on the work that these things necessitate, or else sleeping." I am not saying that this portrait is perfectly applicable to the present day, but I do find that it accords with the mentality of people here, especially as far as work is concerned. For the Chablis grower more often than not is a paragon of professional conscientiousness and duty. The rigour of the climate, the poverty of the soil and the steepness of the slopes constitute a tough school for the grower. Certainly, it is not an easy matter to keep a vineyard anywhere, but in Chablis the difficulties are more numerous – and

In the small hours, a motionless procession of heaters watches over the safety of the vineyard like a surrealist army. ▶

by dint of long familiarity they become well-known old friends, to which the grower becomes firmly attached in the end. When a Chablis producer places a bottle from his choicest plot in front of you on his kitchen table, he is honouring you by inviting you to share the fruit of his labours.

Félix Beau is one of the oldest vignerons in Chablis. Like many of his contemporaries he is also a poet (see the small anthology of Chablis poetry at the back of this book) whose work finds its inspiration in the realities of daily life. One of his most notable poems is the hymn to Chablis sung by a hundred lusty voices every year at the festival of Saint-Vincent:

> Be it our care and hope to store
> Our good – so highly prized,
> Of our fair France that gem so pure,
> A wealth our sires devised.
> Behold the vines with fruit bedecked;
> 'Tis by our toil thereto.
> Let's worthy be of that respect
> Which is the worker's due.

This refrain, coming from the heart of Félix Beau and the mouths of his colleagues, always elicits a performance of true bravura, in the noblest sense of the term.

In Chablis the festival of Saint-Vincent is "mobile". That is to say that it takes place every year in one of the nineteen communes of the region (a description of each of these can be found in the catalogue). The "Saint-Vincent" is a popular event, organized under the aegis of the Brotherhood of the Piliers Chablisiens, founded in 1952. Essentially, the festival's aim is to bring together the producers of the appellation. Taking place in the month of February, it marks the New Year in the life cycle of the vine, and is followed in April or May by the festival of Saint-Cochon, an occasion for a friendly meal worthy of Pantagruel and his disciples, at which the *vin nouveau* is king. Then in the month of August, until quite recently, there was the festival of the vine, with its elegant flower-covered floats.The last Sunday in November is a sort of fair-cum-exhibition open to the public at large in the presence of the *préfet* of the *département*. Diplomas are awarded to the most deserving wine producers (Domaines Laroche won four in 1985), and everyone shares in the good-natured badinage of the Piliers while the applicants are enthroned. A remarkable brass band called "Les Enfants de Chablis", strikes up its resounding music and the "Regain" choral and folk-dance group sing charming polyphonic songs and perform traditional local dances.

Despite the bleak picture of the lowly conditions endured by the vignerons that a realist brush might paint, life in Chablis is lived to the full, following both the rhythm of the seasons and the warm character and good-humoured honesty of the people.

26

The Order of the Piliers Chablisiens (the Pillars of Chablis) is a model of its type, with a strictly ordered hierarchy as follows:

– The *Socles* (Pedestals): Piliers who were the founders of the brotherhood, notably those who gave the initial impetus to the tasting and making known of the wines of the Yonne, and those who have given exceptional services to this or to the region of Chablis in general.

– The *Stylobates*: Piliers, principally hoteliers, restaurateurs, wine-waiters, wine merchants, etc., who undertake to offer their customers – as far as the wines of the Yonne are concerned – only wines of rigorously high standards and, moreover, to affirm their title of Pilier by clearly exhibiting in their establishment the diploma detailing this undertaking. This rank is also granted to officials of various bodies concerned with wine-producing.

– The *Fûts* (Shafts): Piliers, members of the brotherhood.

– The *Frises* (Friezes): Piliers who are honorary members.

The brotherhood is administered by the *Corniche* (Cornice) and directed by the *Chapiteau* (Capital). The *Corniche* consists of:

– Those Piliers with the rank of *Socle*;

– Seven to twelve Piliers elected yearly at the November festival , when the wines of the Yonne are exhibited and tasted.

The *Chapiteau* consists of:

– The Architrave, the Worshipful Master of the brotherhood who is in charge of its activities.

– Two Vice-Architraves, of whom one must be the President of the Federation of Viticulturalists of the Yonne, and the other the President of the Tourist Office of Chablis.

– The Arch-Chancellor, in charge of the brotherhood's external relations.

– The Chancellor, in charge of administering the brotherhood's financial affairs and collecting the annual subscriptions and expenses to be paid by new Piliers.

– The *Chroniqueur* (Chronicler), in charge of recording the history of the brotherhood.

– The *Grand Ordonnateur* (Master of Ceremonies), in charge of arranging the brotherhood's ceremonials.

– The *Grand Orateur* (Orator), in charge of spreading the good word in all matters concerning the brotherhood.

– Two *Grands Echansons* (Butlers), in charge of the choice of wines at the brotherhood's banquets.

– The *Imagier* (Artist-Designer), in charge of drawing up menus and documents; and several *Missi* (Ambassadors), entrusted with all matters concerning public relations.

The following lines are taken from the excellent book by Fernand Woutaz, *Le Grand Livre des confréries des vins de France* (D. Halévy, Paris, 1971): "The atmosphere of these functions is astonishing in its happiness and cor-

diality: social barriers cease to exist; everybody enjoys themselves openly and, as might be imagined, the atmosphere is warm. The *bans* or proclamations become more and more frenetic and the cellar vaults really do seem to reverberate. When everybody is buoyed up, the ceremony begins.

"However, in order to calm people down somewhat, the ceremony is preceded, while the audience remains standing, by a reading of the Pastoral Let-

28

ter of the Archbishop of Mayence who, in about 1563, distributed so many pithy admonishments and warnings :

"Let him who, after the third or fourth jug of wine, feels his reason disturbed to the point of not being able to recognize his wife, children or friends any longer, and ill-treating them, let him then limit himself to two jugs, unless he wishes to offend God and be despised by his neighbour. But let him who, after drinking four, five or six, still remains able to do his work and to conform to the orders of his ecclesiastical and secular superiors, let him then humbly and gratefully drink what God has allowed him to take. But let him beware of over-stepping the limit of six jugs, for it is rare that the infinite goodness of the Lord grants one of His children that favour which He has accorded me, His unworthy servant. I drink eight jugs of wine daily and no one can say that he has seen me yield to unjustified anger or ill-treat my parents or my acquaintances.

"So then, let every one of you, my brothers, strengthen his body and rejoice in mind with the quantity of wine which the Divine Goodness has allowed each of you to absorb."

Here, with laudable concern for historical truth, we should remember another factor: the huge volumes of wine consumed by members of the clergy at a time when religious communities owned the largest and most famous vineyards of Chablis. During the Revolution, as everywhere else in France, ecclesiastical properties were confiscated, divided up and sold at auction. More than a third of the vines belonged to the abbey of Pontigny. They were situated in Valmur, at Les Clos, in Beugnons and in Champlain. The second great property was the Chapitre de Chablis, the principal producer of Les Clos, followed by the group of local chapels which proliferated at Grenouilles, La Chapelle-Saint-Georges, Vaudésir, La Chapelle-Sainte-Marie, Valmur, La Chapelle-Saint-André, etc. There was wholesale appropriation of vines in the *Grands Crus* by the religious communities, who, as everybody knows, have never been slow in finding the road to good wine. One of the popular nineteenth-century prints from Epinal depicting a caricature of a portly monk surrounded by pint pots, is no lie. Burgundian loquaciousness was born in some monastery, between the paternosters and the Ave Marias at all hours of day and night. Since that time the word "spiritual" has taken on a certain ambiguity.

Not only were the monks the largest proprietors of vineyards, but they also had a near monopoly on the presses. So they were able to control their neighbours' production, for the consideration of a cash-down payment. They did business in wine and, as charity begins at home, they drank a lot. Here, a lot really means a lot. When the Archbishop of Mayence shouts from the

---

◄ *At the annual wine fair in Chablis, the principal producers display their wines and compare their respective qualities.*

The Order of the Piliers Chablisiens; a ceremony at Ligny-le-Châtel. ►

rooftops that he drinks eight jugs a day, we are inclined to think that he is exaggerating his capacities. However, if we take the man of God at his word, we must believe he was capable of consuming sixteen pints of wine within twenty-four hours. If we take the smallest measure of a pint, the imperial pint used in Britain, that works out at a daily consumption of more than nine litres. (If the measure were the French pint of the Middle Ages, the volume consumed would have been in the order of fifteen litres!) So we can easily understand how a thirst for owning vineyards became such a driving force in religion. From time to time, there was a clampdown. From the Renaissance onwards, apart from the wine for masses, confined religiously in capacious chalices, the episcopal authorities limited daily consumption to seven pints per head. But holy libations were still allowed and displays of excessive devotion

▲ *One of the Piliers Chablisiens (Monsieur Vocoret) receives Alain Bombard into the brotherhood.*

were common. It was enough to raise one's glass to the health of the Lord, the angels, the Virgin, the saint of the day, the newly deceased and the long-since dead, new-born babes and those about to be born, in order to be absolved from all sin. Only since the Revolution has the popularity of the priesthood declined.

But is all this relevant today? You might be tempted to think that wine's influence has carried me away. Yet when I was studying this region, it was the hold of the clergy which impressed me most strongly. Up to the end of the eighteenth century, nearly everything belonged to them. Traces of this ownership are still in evidence today. The little town of Chablis, which numbers about 2,500 souls, bears witness to this past. Religious buildings are still numerous, although several of them were destroyed at the time of the Revolution. The Chapitre also possessed a large number of the most opulent dwellings: the Obédiencerie is a good example . Saint-Martin is still the parish church. Built on foundations dating from the twelfth century, it has been restored many times, with each succeeding century adding or superimposing its own style. It is the size of a tennis court in area, and the south portal is ornamented with horseshoes, among which you are supposed to be able to recognize those of Joan of Arc's mount, provided you know the size and the original workmanship of the farrier.

The abbey of Pontigny, which was, as we have seen, the largest vineyard owner in Chablis, set up a sort of branch in Chablis itself. A permanent team of twelve monks looked after the assets: vines, cellars, presses and wine-stocks. Thanks to their chroniclers, several documents have come down to us relating the relationships between the different communities, the civil authorities and the peasants. In them we can also find valuable details about the customs of the vine-workers of former times. Thus the former chief priest of Chablis, Messager, tells us of the lease of a vineyard which Jean, the priest of Reigny, granted in 1367 to Perrin Moncoul and his wife. Under the terms of the lease, which concerned three parcels of vines situated in Chablis, in the locality known as Séché, the tenants undertook to carry out the necessary work in accordance with local customs, that is "to remove the soil from the surface roots in alternate years, to train the vines, to prune, to collect and burn the prunings and to hoe deeply every other year", and to pay an annual rent of four sous minted at Tours. In short, a tidy little deal for the Church.

The monasteries of Chablis have always taken a particular delight in the written word. While not all their books of hours and record books have come down to us, it is interesting to note that Chablis had one of the very first printing works in France, forty years after Gutenberg's invention. This was thanks to a pioneer named Pierre Lerouge, whose first published book was *Le Livre de bonnes mœurs* (1478) by the monk Jacques Le Grand. (Today in secular life, another Jacques Legrand carries on his evangelical mission – to which this book is witness!)

With the Revolution, the predominant role of the clergy in the local economy and politics was overthrown amid great commotion. The strength of the religious stranglehold was equalled only by the subsequent violence of the reaction against it in Chablis. In 1793, the Chablis Society of the Friends of Liberty and Equality was set up, a society "of the people" which undertook, not without some friction, to organize the little town, especially in the matters of supplies, revolutionary propaganda and the anti-religious struggle. The extremist "brothers" declared war on religion, overturning crucifixes and persecuting parishioners who remained faithful to the Church. In a fine gesture of patriotic generosity, the members of the society decided to add their own wealth to the church plate confiscated for the Mint. The only exceptions were their *tastevins*, "being necessary to wine producers".

It was at this point that the Chablis vineyards were split up into microplots. Out of concern for justice and equity, they were divided up and distributed like a wedding-cake to feed a multitude of guests. In my opinion, this is the explanation for today's fragmentation of the viticultural land register, which is the principal characteristic of the physiognomy of the land. To give an idea of this, it is only necessary to observe that the *Grands Crus*, which represent a total surface area of scarcely 100 hectares, are split up into some four hundred lots, among which there is only one parcel of more than two hectares and eight of more than one hectare. This tiny scale sharpened the Chablis people's sense of land ownership. For two centuries there have been relatively few changes in the land under vine: "Vines are inherited, not bought." Each parcel is a sacred asset which is handed down from generation to generation, being split up even more when divided up in inheritances. Thus a young vigneron wanting to set up home might turn a blind eye to the fact that Martin's daughter squints, in view of the fact that she has 0.60 hectares in Grenouilles and nearly a hectare in three plots round Vaudésir. Together with the land which has come from his father, there is enough to found a concern, especially because old cousin Marcelline has promised him an interest in her 0.47 hectares in the heart of Les Preuses. And for the wedding, Uncle Bill, brother of Martin's daughter's mother, will provide all the wine one could wish for.

This also explains demands for appellations to be extended in the interests of a more rational viticulture. Many Chablis people can be compared to top dress-designers, who every year make their name with their finest creations of *haute couture* (hand-sewn, stitch by stitch), but who may make their money from the more easily mass-produced 'prêt-à-porter' collections. "In fact this is the case with several recently created large wine-producing undertakings in

---

◄ *The town of Chablis is rich in reminders of its past, here reflected in the waters of the Serein. For several centuries, the little river has been channelled through a quiet reach along which families used to do their washing. There were also numerous flour-mills, both up- and downstream.*

Chablis, with a holding of 45 hectares in Viviers, and another more or less equivalent in Maligny", confirms Gérald Jack Gilbank in his masterly study *Les Vignobles de qualité du sud-ouest du Bassin Parisien.* And he goes on: "These large-sized holdings come about from recent purchases of land which had been left fallow for several decades. They are often on the fringes of vineyards, where competition for land has been less keen. Everywhere else, it is a question of reorganization of land: parcels deriving from inherited land and those from bought land create a unit, sometimes ill-assorted, which corresponds neither to the wishes of the grower nor to the requirements of modern techniques." Later in his analysis, Gérald Gilbank offers a complementary explanation for the splitting up of parcels in any one undertaking: the commercial attraction which they represent. It is the old story of the chicken and the egg. As the land of the *Grands Crus* has reached saturation point, it is impossible to plant new vines. The growers have thus sought other land and, having found it, have increased the range of their products, so enlarging their commercial scope. History can always be written in several ways. I have always liked the two descriptions of the Battle of Fontenoy: "Messieurs les Anglais

▲ *The panorama over the* Grands Crus *is one of the most beautiful viticultural landscapes in France.*

(*comma*) fire first (*row of dots*)" was the invitation the Count of Auteroche is said to have politely extended on May 11, 1745. The other version goes that as soon as the fiery commander of Maréchal de Saxe's reconnaissance troops observed the vanguard of the English guards commanded by Lord Charles Hay, he turned to his own men and shouted to them: "Messieurs (*comma*) Les Anglais (*exclamation marks*) Fire first (*salvo of exclamation marks*)". Thus it was that the French emptied their muskets, decimating the first of the English lines. Could it be that the famous battle took place at Fontenay and not Fontenoy? This is the opinion of certain historians from Chablis. In which case, the fearlessness of the Count of Auteroche could be explained by a good bumper of Preuses. By and large, history is one huge question mark. For myself, I think that the Chablis people most probably tried to increase the size of their vineyards from a simple, human desire to improve the family inheritance, though I have no string of academic references to support this theory. The diversification of their production came about from the increasing disparity of the land on which they had their vines. Not the other way round. But land for new plantations had to be found. Thus started the Kimmeridgian wars, to which we shall return later on.

But it is true that for an honest man from Chablis the ability to offer a few drops from the Côte de Valmur at the head of his list is the diamond in his crown. It remains to be seen how the stone is to be set or mounted. It

Production of Chablis wines in hectolitres

Year	Petit-Chablis	Chablis	1er Cru	Grand Cru	Total
1948	3 250	2 300	4 710	564	10 824
1949	2 659	2 071	4 202	599	9 531
1950	6 966	4 321	8 746	1 040	21 073
1951	3 812	2 705	3 902	32	10 451
1952	3 708	3 291	5 749	687	13 435
1953	1 972	1 430	1 974	104	5 480
1954	5 171	4 229	7 108	677	17 185
1955	6 254	4 772	7 824	671	19 521
1956	2 808	2 238	3 302	386	8 734
1957	600	355	735	1	1 691
1958	2 302	2 647	5 469	655	11 073
1959	3 190	6 590	6 840	760	17 380
1960	2 991	7 426	6 689	681	17 787
1961	2 372	5 052	5 359	672	13 455
1962	4 202	9 393	9 868	1 111	24 574
1963	5 044	11 956	11 625	1 389	30 014
1964	3 721	9 240	9 722	1 340	24 023
1965	3 520	9 295	8 437	1 240	22 492
1966	5 180	13 000	12 000	1 895	30 075
1967	3 930	9 200	8 770	1 420	23 320
1968	4 050	15 752	7 894	1 485	29 181
1969	2 430	8 145	7 520	1 720	19 815
1970	6 415	17 770	14 035	2 670	40 890
1971	3 879	11 778	8 984	356	24 997
1972	5 283	16 245	11 233	2 295	35 056
1973	8 001	21 859	14 849	3 492	48 201
1974	8 309	28 282	10 956	2 685	50 232
1975	9 543	29 443	15 591	3 907	58 484
1976	8 384	31 934	16 721	4 444	61 483
1977	4 147	16 958	26 251	1 856	49 212
1978	2 332	25 178	17 731	3 850	49 091
1979	7 989	66 126	33 988	6 124	114 227
1980	5 959	46 601	25 491	5 113	82 564
1981	1 723	22 749	15 686	2 864	43 022
1982	7 375	69 682	33 775	6 075	116 907
1983	8 724	83 260	41 359	6 772	140 115
1984	5 161	68 129	35 603	5 617	114 510
1985	6 218	65 294	25 650	2 693	99 855
1986	5 811	65 602	32 339	4 676	108 428
1987	9 673	82 228	34 849	5 060	131 810
1988	10 693	91 827	36 815	4 920	144 255

could be matched with other precious jewels, taken from the *Premiers Crus*, or else with a few good quality zircons coming from "Chablis" appellation – or else more whimsical semi-precious stones, charming none the less, in the style of "Petit-Chablis". I dare say that there is as big a difference in quality between a Valmur and a Petit-Chablis as there is between a Margaux and a (plain) Bordeaux. But as a general rule, when it comes to buying a "Chablis" the price, as always, is a pretty sure guide.

In order to consider the statistics objectively, here, in round figures, are the total areas of each of the four appellations and the average volumes produced (based on the 1987 harvest):

Chablis Grand Cru	100 hectares	5,000 hectolitres
Chablis Premier Cru	660 hectares	35,000 hectolitres
Chablis	1,400 hectares	80,000 hectolitres
Petit-Chablis	160 hectares	10,000 hectolitres

The yields per hectare also reveal a corresponding and logical progression in quality. Still in round figures, the average is 50 hectolitres for the *Grand Cru*, 53 hectolitres for the *Premier Cru*, 57 hectolitres for the Chablis AOC and 60 hectolitres for Petit-Chablis. Although the spread is not very wide, each with very few exceptions has its proper place in the hierarchy of appellations. It is also clear that, frost or hail permitting, the yields are abundant. They were nearly three times less a century ago. As for the growth in the area under production, there has been an increase of 300 per cent over the last twenty-five years. For ten years now, problems associated with the weather have been much better controlled, allowing the viti-vinicultural economy to progress at a good cruising speed. Formerly, successive harvests could show wide disparities, as the table opposite shows.

Today, distance is no longer considered an obstacle to enlarging a vineyard. A quarter of an hour or even half an hour by car or tractor to cultivate a large parcel of land is no longer an inconvenience. The Chablis vineyards extend over four intercommunal sectors:
1. Maligny-Lignorelles-Beine, comprising the communes of Maligny, Lignorelles, Beine, La Chapelle-Vaupelteigne, Ligny-le-Châtel and Villy;
2. Chablis, comprising the communes of Fyé, Milly and Poinchy, recently merged with Chablis, and, last of all, the commune of Fontenay-près-Chablis;
3. Chichée-Fleys, comprising the communes of Chemilly-sur-Serein, Chichée, Fleys, Béru, Rameau, Poilly-sur-Serein and Viviers;
4. Courgis and Préhy.

There was once a village in lower Burgundy called Chablis, which day and night watched with love over its celebrated slopes. (Behind is the hillside of Les Lys). ▸

Since the new delimitation of Chablis in 1976, there has no longer been any problem regarding availability of land and thus the possibility of creating new vineyards. Apart from the area of the *Grands Crus*, which is planted to the full, the three other appellations have considerable reserves to call on, to the order of 3,500 hectares for Chablis *Premier Cru* and Chablis combined and about 1,800 hectares for Petit-Chablis. However, the INAO (Institut Na-

tional des Appellations d'Origine) has granted permission for new plantations very sparingly. Over the last ten years, the growers have been presented
with a paradox. On the one hand, the authorities extended the boundaries of
the AOC (with the exception, of course, of Chablis *Grand Cru*), and on the
other they took an extremely restrictive line on each annual quota for new
plantations. It seems that the two levels of decision-making, the one theoreti-

cal and the other essentially practical, were not coordinated at the outset. In June 1977, the two federations of the Chablis appellation raised their voices loud enough to make themselves heard by the minister of agriculture. The growers had been invited by their respective town halls to register their requests for authorization to plant, subject to two constraints: that the overall quota should not exceed 75 hectares and that any one person should not ask for more than 2 hectares per vineyard. The total amount of the requests came to 81 hectares; the authorities, fearing that they might be obliged to provide a breakdown, intimidated by the excess production of ordinary table-wines and harassed by the complaints concerning the new delimitations, turned a deaf ear and in a superb display of solidarity refused all 81 hectares. This was more than the growers of Chablis could stand: "The attention of the minister should first of all be called to the fact that such a brutal measure, taken in respect of vineyards which for several years have been in the throes of increasing their plantations very rapidly, and this at the very wish of the public authorities, would create hostile reactions and material difficulties which cannot be ignored. Such a measure would create shocking inequalities between people who over the recent years have benefited from authorizations to plant extensively, sometimes on land of little viticultural value, and the majority of the growers who yearly increase their vineyard only by some quarter of an acre and have an imperative need to continue to do so regularly." Without passing judgement on the cogency of these arguments – which in fact seem to me to be logically acceptable – I give you my personal impression: this written speech exhales the very spirit of republican rural France. Time was when no government could be formed and continue to exist without the support of the huge numbers of wine producers, provided they derived a (certain) satisfaction from it! A certain amount of concentration is required to understand this extract from the response: "The one prudent measure which the present situation of the delimitations of these vineyards can dictate to the minister of agriculture should in our opinion be to grant only to Petit-Chablis authorization for plantations requested for lands whose identification in the Chablis area is not yet finally determined; and to Chablis the requested authorization for lands whose identification among the *Premiers Crus* is likewise not determined finally." In other words, there has been a levelling out from the bottom. None the less, this chain of events presents an attractive picture of the ripples and swirls which occur in that charming little French river called the Serein. I have simply drawn attention to it, almost at random, extracting it from the appellation's impressive dossier, not in order to put it in a show-case but rather to display it among postcards of the region. Here are a few figures to complement the discussion above (see the table opposite).

All in all, the vineyards of Chablis together make an excellent production unit. I personally approve of the recent review of *climats** with the *Premier Cru* appellation. If in recent years marketing trends have pushed Chablis to

42

Commune	Chablis Grand Cru		Chablis 1er Cru		Chablis		Petit-Chablis		Total of the 4 AOCs	
	hl	ha	hl	ha	hl	ha	hl	ha	hl	ha
Beine			2 000	33.65	6 297	106.73	537	9.33	8 834	149.71
Bernouil					60	1.01			60	1.01
Béru			111	2.45	1 618	27.24	17	.29	1 746	29.98
Bleigny-le-Carreau					138	2.30			138	2.30
Chablis	4 425	81.37	19 015	322.64	20 790	358.92	1 389	25.96	45 619	788.89
Chemilly-sur-Serein			111	1.88	4 793	80.16	507	8.63	5 411	90.67
Chichée			1 211	21.95	5 461	98.38	46	.89	6 718	121.22
Chitry			671	11.22	1 065	19.16	401	6.70	2 137	37.08
Collan-Rameau					128	3.70	36	.59	164	4.29
Courgis			1 422	24.49	4 955	93.63	141	2.35	6 518	120.47
Epineuil			16	.25	347	6.05	60	1	422	7.30
Fleys			2 059	34.88	2 765	48.34	51	.84	4 875	84.06
Fontenay-près-Chablis	547	10.13	2 049	34.25	4 123	70	1 320	22.04	8 039	136.42
La Chapelle-Vaupelteigne	88	2	2 013	33.84	4 843	81.04	326	5.44	7 270	122.32
Lignorelles			619	10.73	6 532	126.39	3 246	47.71	10 397	184.83
Ligny-le-Châtel			181	2.96	55	.92	10	.25	246	4.13
Maligny			2 479	42.35	6 555	111.71	814	14.54	9 848	168.60
Poilly-sur-Serein					641	10.70			641	10.70
Saint-Bris-le-Vineux			502	8.44	405	7.07	78	1.30	985	16.70
Saint-Cyr-les-Colons-Préhy			162	2.74	3 736	62.72	163	3.01	4 061	68.47
Serrigny			18	.30	278	4.70			296	5
Tonnerre							350	6.03	350	6.03
Varennes			44	.74					44	.74
Villy					1 851	30.83	164	2.73	2 015	33.56
Viviers			167	2.80	4 792	79.91	17	.30	4 976	83.01
Total	5 060	93.50	34 849	592.56	82 228	1 431.61	9 673	159.93	131 810	2 277.60

the fore, it seems to me that giving the *Premiers Crus* more individuality is a good idea. It takes all sorts to make a world. In the face of foreign competition, especially Californian, which takes unfair advantage of the name of Chablis, it is a good thing to raise standards rather than lower them. And for the wine-lover, it is an entirely understandable desire to want to discover the different characters of the *crus* from one area to another. My pilgrimages in the Chablis area have convinced me of this. And of this I can assure you: if the *Grands Crus* represent the ancient and glorious nobility of Chablis, the *Premiers Crus* form an aristocracy which is a credit to them and entirely to be recommended. And their production capacity is on a reasonable and appropriate scale for world-wide distribution.

Chablis is a wine for oysters...
... born from their shells

"Dry, limpid, perfumed, lively and light."

Might it be Pierre Poupon and not Raymond Dumay who has just been speaking? By the way, I have so far neglected to tell you that Chablis is a white wine. This is not as silly as it sounds: it is the whitest of white wines but with nuances and subtle plays of colour. With diamonds, the finest quality is detectable by their "blue-whiteness". With Chablis, it is by its "green-whiteness". Chablis wine is never yellow, unless through age, a mistake or even a defect; or worse still, because it is a fake. Its rare clarity doubtless contributed to its original popularity. Before even identifying its taste, you could distinguish it from other wines by its colour which, from the Middle Ages, appeared divine to the men of God. It was pre-eminently the wine used at mass, for it symbolized extreme purity. Its resistance to oxidation enabled it to be kept for a long time without any adulteration or other "sacrilegious" treatment, and its natural limpidity for long appeared supernatural.

It had already acquired this reputation in the ninth century when Charles the Bald, who was celebrating Christmas at Auxerre in the year of grace 867,

◄ *On this Portland limestone, herbicides are virtually unnecessary.*

A view of the Chablis vineyards between Béru and Viviers. The vines enjoy heights. ►

donned a superb robe, beside which any cardinal's would have paled, to place a superb gift at the feet of the Reverend Prior of Saint-Martin de Tours. With his enormous white beard, he must have looked like the first person to dress up as Father Christmas.

But to return to this magnificent present: it was, we read, his *cella nomine Capleiam*. For the time being, we are not going to bother ourselves with deep etymological considerations. *Nomine Capleiam* means simply "by the name of

Chablis". But what does *cella* mean? Here the affair moves into the realm of farce. All the religious authorities who have brought their learning to bear on the matter have translated it in the strict sense accorded to it by the Roman architect Vitruvius, that is to say, a chapel or sanctuary in a temple. It is quite clear that this was in no way Christian and that Vitruvius used the word in a technical sense to mean a significant annexe in purpose if not literally in its capacity. In vernacular Latin *cella* meant the place for storing foodstuffs such as cereals, oil, fruits – and wine. The word is patently the forerunner of the French word *cellier* and the English *cellar*. In this way, monkish prudery cast a veil over the nature of Charles the Bald's present. I arrive in time to restore Chablis' history to its true dignity. It was indeed a cellar of wine, the best in the area according to historians. To justify the offering, Charles the Bald had had a little chapel constructed, consecrated to Saint Loup (Wolf). So with this *cella*, everybody's conscience was cleared. And Saint Loup was remembered with affection in the area for, as Bishop of Troyes, he had defended the marches of Burgundy inch by inch against Attila. Since that time there has scarcely been any need for herbicides in the vineyards although, according to some, the Kimmeridgian *terroir* might have contributed in a more practical way to this.

The monks of Saint-Martin de Tours took possession of the "chapel" and were only too happy to celebrate mass in it. At that time, there were practically no vineyard proprietors among the laity. That is no longer the case today. The proof is the following extract from the *Chablis Républicain*. This satirical newspaper, "which used to appear from time to time on a Wednesday in Chablis", upheld the tradition of the anticlerical *sans-culottes*. In its edition of December 6, 1972, the editor-in-chief crossed pens with his great contemporary, the daily newspaper the *Yonne Républicaine*, which had published a report on the recent Chablis wine fair-cum-exhibition in an article by Monsieur de Crancé: "What Monsieur de Crancé has yet to learn before he may come to work at the *Chablis Républicain* is that many vignerons belong to the laity. Yes Sir, even though they may have been educated by priests. So, then, to announce that the wine festival of Chablis will begin 'on Sunday, as soon as mass is finished', has irritated the republican element among the vignerons. They had already attacked Madame Villemet (the local correspondent of the *Yonne Républicaine*) because she had written that the civil festival of Saint-Vincent would begin with the mass. So now they wonder what they have done to the Almighty that these blessed clowns at the *Yonne Républicaine* should want them to attend mass at all costs before the festival. In short, all this is a mass of crass nonsense which has been amassed and ventilated simply in order to be able to say that the 1972 Chablis wine fair was an unholy war to rival the holy day of August 15." Chablis has come a long way from the days when its wine was reserved for holy communion! The wine has not changed. It is the canon and the rites which have been modified.

But let us go back to the end of the ninth century to see the monks of Saint-Martin de Tours at work. They then reigned over Chablis and their reputation spread throughout the kingdom. The counts of Champagne took them under their protection in order that they might be able to devote themselves to their pious – that is to say, fruitful – activities. But sooner or later the price of glory has to be paid. In commercial terms, it is known as competition. In the year 1114 came a thunderbolt from the blue as Tonnerre, a town to the east of Chablis, watched the new order of monks called Cistercians passing through

48

on their way to found their abbey at Pontigny. They too lost no time in planting vines. The "unholy war" of the Chablis AOC had only just begun. It still goes on, with secular battle-cries of course. And if Pontigny is excluded from the appellation today, the tourist pamphlets of Chablis remember its part in history in their own way: "Well worth a visit, beyond the vineyards of Chablis, yet very close, is the abbey of Pontigny, the second of the four daughters of Cîteaux, founded in the twelfth century." But let the tourist beware: today he can take photos, but not buy wine!

The Cistercians exploited their young talent and creative ardour to the full. They created vineyards which surpassed those of the monks in Saint-Martin, basking in their prosperity in the village of Chablis, eight miles to the south. When they woke up in Saint-Martin, it was too late. The chroniclers of the day unfortunately do not relate all the details of this conflict. It is highly possible that some of the region's place names date from this time: Tue-Villain, Chape-Guerre, L'Homme-Mort, etc. Four years later, weary of battle, they came to terms in order to try and live together in peace. The chapter of Saint-Martin de Chablis was suitably rewarded, for it was to receive rent from the lands under its provostship which had been colonized by the monks of Pontigny. In 1151 the Count of Troyes, to whom the supervision of the territory fell, declared that he wished personally to take charge of it. He trimmed it down

▲ *It is becoming increasingly rare for estates to harvest completely by hand. Above: William Fèvre's team of harvesters.*

49

on both sides. But after him, the lords of Montréal displayed more interest. In 1181, Anséric II, lord of Montréal and seneschal of Burgundy, put himself in the good graces of the abbot of Pontigny by presenting him with a vineyard he owned in Chablis "whose white wine may be kept for a long time". At this news, the abbot of Saint-Martin issued a foaming bull whose contents were to the effect that Pontigny could own no more than 36 *arpents* of vines in Chablis (approximately 15 hectares). The men to the north responded with the promotion of La Moutonne, whose wines enjoyed an unprecedented success. Even today, this name commands a premium over many other *Grands Crus*. Its label now adorns bottles from the two and a quarter hectares owned by the Beaune firms of Bichot and Drouhin in the Vaudésir region. The publicity of former years claimed that this wine had exceptional diuretic powers. Some claimed that those who drank it began at once to "pee like pigs".

The chaplains of Saint-Martin de Tours ruminated over their vengeance for some time. In 1215 they decided to buy the finest patch of vines belonging to Guy de Montréal. The latter, who was not a venal character, pushed the price up to 2,000 livres! The pious monks delved into the collection boxes and coffers to rake together 1,300 livres. It was not enough. The father in charge of the monastic accounts went to the prior and advised him to convert the gold covering the high altar into hard cash. "Invest in the gold of the land!", he told him. The prior did not require much persuasion and agreed to strip the altar to provide the balance. "Our Lord was born on the straw", he had the novices sing, to remind them of life's asperity. "Long live the good wine of Chablis," they intoned in reply, "it is bottled gold." Since this (entirely true) episode, Chablis has been known as the "Golden Gate to Burgundy".

If the regular clergy from far and wide owned most of the vines in Chablis, from the thirteenth century smallholdings began to be counted in hundreds. Some 1,328 belonged to 450 proprietors managing 500 *arpents* (nearly 200 hectares). Two hundred years later, there were about seven hundred "people bringing their harvest" to the town presses. Without wishing to pre-empt well-meaning socialism, the wine co-operative system was an invention of the clergy. In the seventeenth century, 1,600 *arpents* were in production. The writer Boileau had a famous vineyard near Tonnerre. He perhaps found his inspiration for *Le Lutrin* there. In the eighteenth century Gaudin, the canon and senior priest of Chablis, conducted a regular correspondence with the beautiful former patroness of Jean Jacques Rousseau, Louise Tardieu d'Esclavelles, the lady of La Live d'Epinay. He expressed his feelings thus: "My wine is heady; when you drink it, it perfumes and delights the throat and leaves a sweet odour of truffles." What gallantry!

The wines of Chablis have always provoked torrents of words to describe them. Doctor Guyot has bequeathed a delicious description to the memory of any Chablisien who has the slightest smattering of learning, in his report to Napoleon III indicating the qualities of the best wines of the Empire: "The wines of Chablis occupy one of the highest places among the white wines of France. Spirituous, without making themselves felt on the mind, they have body, finesse and a charming perfume. Their whiteness and limpidity are remarkable. But they are particularly to be noted for their hygienic and digestive qualities and the lively stimulation, benign and full of lucidity, which they impart to the intelligence. Despite the reputation they have justifiably enjoyed, and this for a long time, their real value is, I think, even greater than their fame." This commentary is known by heart to every wine producer in Chablis, who will not fail to make reference to it. Even Pierre Poupon, a purist with a rather peremptory approach to Burgundy wines, includes it in his repertoire. Yet when he quotes it he leaves out the passage about the "digestive" and intellectual qualities. I suspect Pierre Poupon of having pledged himself body and soul to the wine of Meursault! I will give Jacques Benoit, an excellent writer on gastronomy for the *Presse de Montréal*, the task of replying to him. This article appeared on August 17, 1985: "The region of Chablis produces, as everybody knows, one of the most extraordinary white wines in France. A wine light in colour with hints of green, very dry, rather light with discreet mineral and saline after-flavours. Many people (including me) prefer it for example to Meursault, which is more full-bodied and mellow. One thing about it which is rather rare for white wines is that it is capable of ageing for up to about ten years, sometimes more, which makes it a particularly worthwhile purchase."

Here I must put in a word to underline this special feature: a white wine which can age! Already at the end of this century we have got out of the habit of leaving red wines for years to mature, let alone whites. Yet it is quite certain that the wines of Chablis are particularly suitable for ageing and that their first attack can sometimes make you grind your teeth. Pierre Poupon backs me up: "The wines which have just finished fermenting are still young and very acid. When you first taste them, they can make you turn pale and give a little shiver. But they will turn out well, their youth changing into vivacity and their acidity into freshness, both combining to exhale an impalpable perfume of iris" (*Vignes et Jours*, Ed. Jean Dupin, Beaune, 1963). How true this is! And how right the authorities have been to empty the bistros of Paris for some years now of these "infant" Chablis, fresh from the press, which have no other virtue than that of being an acceptable verjuice! Having said this, we shall return later to the *vin bourru*, or new wine.

Yes, the best Chablis must be aged, preferably in wood. Like their red-blooded brothers from Burgundy or Bordeaux, the time spent in the wood of a cask greatly helps the process of maturation. After a year or two in oak and then as long again in the bottle, Chablis develops like a child who can at last talk. And its conversation is marvellous, for those who know how to listen. Hugh Johnson adds his pinch of British salt to the subject: "To be on form, they need at least three (and sometimes even up to ten) years' ageing in the

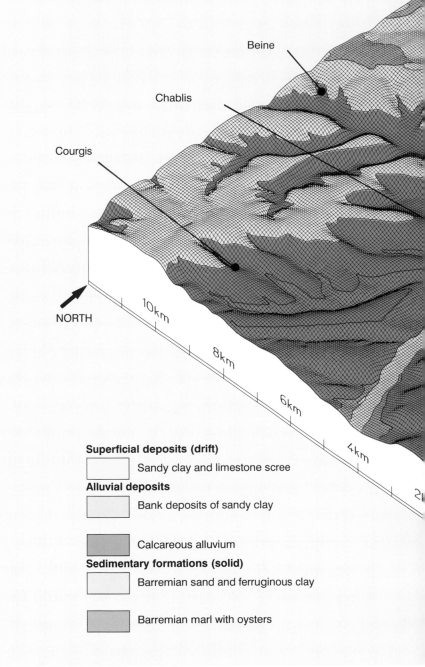

Regions of Chablis
Geology and Land formation

Beine

Chablis

Courgis

NORTH

10km

8km

6km

4km

2k

Superficial deposits (drift)

Sandy clay and limestone scree

Alluvial deposits

Bank deposits of sandy clay

Calcareous alluvium

Sedimentary formations (solid)

Barremian sand and ferruginous clay

Barremian marl with oysters

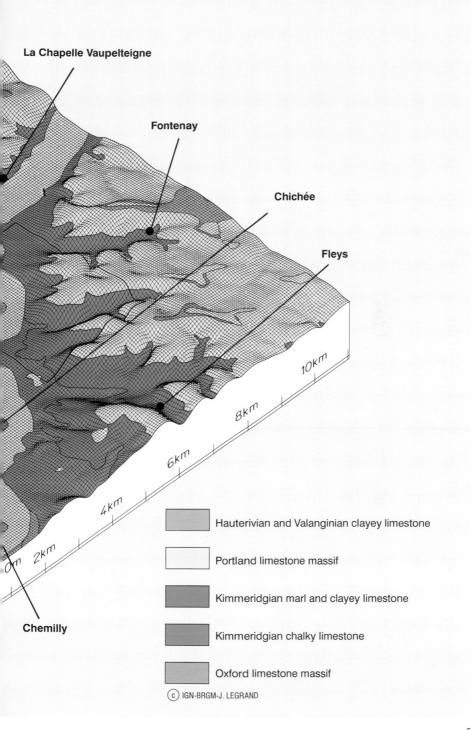

La Chapelle Vaupelteigne

Fontenay

Chichée

Fleys

10km

8km

6km

4km

2km

0m

Chemilly

Hauterivian and Valanginian clayey limestone

Portland limestone massif

Kimmeridgian marl and clayey limestone

Kimmeridgian chalky limestone

Oxford limestone massif

© IGN-BRGM-J. LEGRAND

bottle. Those which are matured in wood (the minority) live longer and better. The aroma and flavour they develop are the very quintessence of an evanescent characteristic which will escape you if you drink only young Chablis all the time. I can define it only in this way: a combination of a flavour of apple and hay with a hint of boiled sweets and a mineral after-flavour which seems to have come from the entrails of the earth." Hugh! dear friend, spare me the boiled sweets. I have never tasted one, nor do I wish to. But otherwise your overall analysis seems to me to be exact, and especially, I repeat especially, that mineral flavour coming from "the entrails of the earth", detected by the palates of all good tasters. I now call on the testimony of the late Alexis Lichine; I do not know if he ever sucked boiled sweets, but on the other hand he declares that he has never eaten flint, despite his powerful jaws: "The great *crus* of Chablis have the greatest distinction and character with, moreover, what is known as a flavour of flint. Seeing that I have never tasted flint, I suppose that this metaphorical term means a biting flavour. A great Chablis *cru* of a good vintage which has been vinified correctly presents a strange combination of austere vigour and hardness as well as the elegant fruit imparted by the chardonnay and the pebbly soil lying over limestone."

"The pebbly soil lying over limestone". This is where it becomes complicated. For the delimitation of the Chablis vineyards has created repercussions, sometimes picturesque or unexpected, sometimes technical or political, sometimes a war between parishes and boroughs, sometimes arguments between experts or inflammatory pamphlets. Some wrote while drinking, others drank while writing. Some drank without writing, others wrote without drinking. Some got up at night to drink, others to write. Some could not sleep and others were asleep on their feet because of it. Some stood down out of fatigue, while others sprang to their feet in rage.

Under the Restoration there existed a circle of epicureans. These people knew what good living means. At one time, their president was the Chevalier de Piis, the founder of the Vaudeville Theatre, famous for the pomp of his receptions and his poetic gems:

> Ne'er fades from memory's span
> Dry Chablis, bright and clear;
> From out whose charms it teaches man
> The oyster to revere.

This disciple of Epicurus did not realize how true his conceit was. For the wine of Chablis is destined to partner oysters. The vines draw their iodine character, their sustenance, from oyster beds situated within the geological stratum

---

◄ *Seen from Montée de Tonnerre, the slopes of Blanchot dominate the valley of the Serein. In the background is part of the village of Chablis.*

..."*a mineral after-flavour which seems to have come from the entrails of the earth.*" Apart from Exogyra virgula, *the main constituent of Kimmeridgian terroir* (see below), *the Chablis subsoil is also rich in fossils and minerals: a real collector's paradise.*

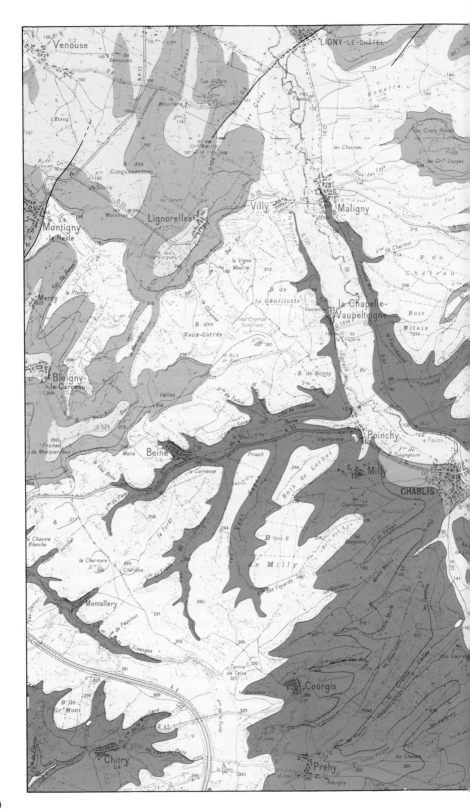

60

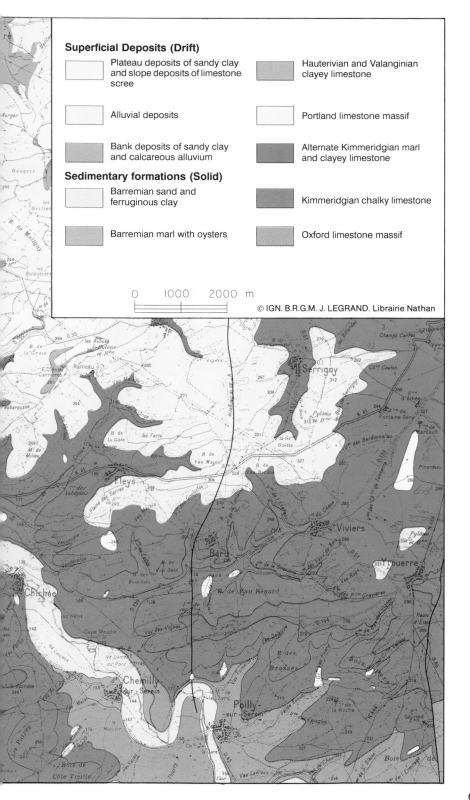

Superficial Deposits (Drift)

Plateau deposits of sandy clay and slope deposits of limestone scree

Alluvial deposits

Bank deposits of sandy clay and calcareous alluvium

Sedimentary formations (Solid)

Barremian sand and ferruginous clay

Barremian marl with oysters

Hauterivian and Valanginian clayey limestone

Portland limestone massif

Alternate Kimmeridgian marl and clayey limestone

Kimmeridgian chalky limestone

Oxford limestone massif

0   1000   2000 m

© IGN. B.R.G.M. J. LEGRAND. Librairie Nathan

years later on the grapevine, never having seen a single paper on the matter."
Once, when he was on the spot examining the local limestone, haversack on back and hammer in hand, he realized that he was being watched by a grower. Striking up a conversation with him, he asked:
"According to what criteria did the vignerons site their vineyards?"
The man gave a wry smile.
"Ah, good sir, the people of old did not possess your knowledge but they had a palate!"
This vigneron did not know that Serge Debrand-Passard has as great a love for samples of *Exogyra virgula* as he has for any Chablis *Premier Cru*.

In my humble opinion, it would be highly desirable for the branch of the INAO responsible for delimitations to get in touch with the geologists at the BRGM (Bureau de Recherches Géologiques et Minières) , who have at their disposal the most up-to-date equipment and the latest technology. Without going into details, I would imagine that if these two specialist organizations were to pool their knowledge the results would considerably and surprisingly extend our understanding of vineyards. A new science would be born: geoviticulture. Everybody is waiting for it. So what are they waiting for?

It would be instructive here to look back over the last hundred years of Chablis' development, though mentioning only the most important dates.
1886. The authentic Chablis vineyards stretch out over barely a dozen communes concentrated on the hillsides, that is on the belt of Kimmeridgian clay chalk, on either side of the valley of the Serein and the many little valleys round Chablis. The vines spill out from this commune onto the best neighbouring hillsides, notably round Milly, Poinchy, Beine (Côte de Trœsmes), La Chapelle (Côte de Fourchaume), Fontenay, Fyé (Côte de Montée de Tonnerre), Fleys (Côte de Mont de Milieu), Chichée, Courgis, and Préhy.
1887. The first evidence of the phylloxera louse is noted in Chablis.
1893. Rapid encroachment of phylloxera. Total destruction of the vineyards.
1897. The vineyards are restored with American root-stock.
1898. A local wine merchant buys up large quantities of Spanish wine which he resells as "Chablis". This word at the time meant a dry white wine from the carafe or over the counter. In this way it distances itself from any geographical connotation, becoming simply a "generic" appellation. The development of business by rail is largely responsible for fraud concerning the origin of the wines, the stamp of the railway station from which they are forwarded serving as a certificate of origin.
1904. Monsieur Rousseaux, director of the agricultural research station of the Yonne and Monsieur Chappaz, professor of agriculture for the department, publish a treatise on the Chablis vineyards. For the first time, formal reference is made to Kimmeridgian soil : "The wines of the Chablis region as such grow on soil made up of Kimmeridgian marl; consequently, the study of the

terrain of the Chablis vineyards is to some extent a study of the soils and substrata of Kimmeridgian origin." The expression "of Kimmeridgian origin" was to prove extremely unfortunate, giving rise to three-quarters of a century of confusion.

1908. On May 24, the Union des propriétaires-vignerons de Chablis takes action against fraud, creating the first "Certificat d'origine de Chablis ". The bungs of the casks are covered with sealing-wax before being dispatched: red for the wines of pure beaunois stock (chardonnay) and green for lesser stock. The stamp of the Union, a registered trademark, certifies the seal. In response to the initiative of Monsieur Long-Depaquit, a substantial figure in Chablis, one hundred and forty producers join the Union.

1919. The first law is passed concerning *appellations d'origine*, based on the principle of quantitative control. A commission combining viticulturalists and wine merchants, at the behest of the prefect of the Yonne, is given the task of proposing an administrative delimitation of the Chablis *crus*. The Chablis producers begin by marking out the *Grands Crus* : Moutonne, Les Clos, Vaudésir, Grenouilles, Valmur and Blanchot, and put forward the view "that only wines from pinot chardonnay grapes, commonly called *beaunois*, harvested in the vineyards of Chablis and surrounding communes – Fontenay-près-Chablis, Fyé, Milly, Poinchy, Chichée, Courgis, Fleys (*climat* of Mont de Milieu), La Chapelle-Vaupelteigne (*climat* of Fourchaume) and Beine (*climat* of Trœsmes) – ought to have the right to the Chablis appellation. And that white wines harvested in the same vineyards and *climats*, but coming from vines other than beaunois, should be called Petit-Chablis. But the joint commission of the Yonne grants the Chablis appellation to all beaunois wines coming from the canton of Chablis and all the surrounding cantons (Auxerre, Vermenton, Noyers, Coulanges-la-Vineuse), that is, virtually the whole of the *département*.

1920. Appealing against this decision, the Burgundy joint commission proposes three appellations:

"Grands Vins de Chablis" for the *crus* produced by the growers of Chablis;

"Chablis Village Supérieur" for the beaunois wines from the canton of Chablis, plus the communes of Ligny-le-Châtel, Lignorelles, Maligny, Villy, Beine, Viviers and Chemilly-sur-Serein;

"Chablis Village" for other white wines from all these communes (this appellation was never applied).

The same year, a law case reveals that barmen in Paris are selling any old white wine from lower Burgundy under the name of Chablis.

1921. Determined to police itself, the Union des propriétaires-vignerons de Chablis grants the "Chablis Village" appellation to all producers of pure and unadulterated beaunois in every commune of the canton of Chablis, plus four communes of the canton of Ligny-le-Châtel and three communes of the canton of Tonnerre.

1923. A decision of the court of Tonnerre names Messieurs Rousseaux, Lustan and Chavard as qualified to establish the extent of the Kimmeridgian terrain over the commune of Béru. The co-operative called "La Chablisienne"is founded.

1929. After more than five years of litigation, the "Petit-Chablis" and "Chablis Village" appellations are forbidden. It is no longer a question of reference to the Kimmeridgian nature of the land and the court refers only to the administrative delimitations of the communes, the chardonnay variety and "local tried and tested practices".

1937-8. As everywhere else in France, the Chablis vineyards go through a grave economic crisis. The *feuillette* of 132 litres, the price of which had reached 1,800 francs in 1929, falls to 220 francs in 1934. "From now on, there is no Chablis society dominating all the vineyards by virtue of the size of its properties and its commercial superiority" (Gérald Jack Gilbank, op. cit.). It is now that the important laws regulating the French AOCs are drawn up. The decree of January 13, 1938, drafted on the instructions of Georges Chappaz, who has become Inspector General for Agriculture, stipulates that "the only white wines to have the right to the Chablis appellation are those which, fulfilling the conditions cited hereafter, have been harvested on the following terrains, with the exception of parcels not situated on Kimmeridgian" (there follows the list of the twenty communes admitted in 1923). Article 2 stipulates that the wines must come exclusively from pinot chardonnay.

1938-42. A battle of experts to determine the delimitation of the Kimmeridgian terrain. Professors Rousseaux, Lemoine and Chaput disagree as to the exact definition of the geological phenomenon. Although theoretically established on paper, the Chablis AOC cannot be effectively applied. The INA0 remains uncommitted and there is widespread disagreement.

1943. In order to calm certain people down, the INAO creates a "Petit-Chablis" appellation, which even today President William Fèvre calls an "unfortunate error", for although the adjective *petit* (little) is often used to convey the idea of affection, it does not reflect the splendour and extent of the Chablis terrain. But at least this term defined a basic minimum quality with the name of Chablis.

1956. After fifteen turbulent but unproductive years, the INAO sets up a new commission of experts. The area producing AOC Chablis is extended by 500 hectares. From this moment, the vineyards thrive and marketing of the wine blossoms.

1967. The classifying and delimitation of the *Premiers Crus*. The growers of Maligny are not prepared to accept the injustice done to them by the suppression of the "Chablis" appellation. The conflict starts up again.

1971. At the suggestion of the INAO, the Minister of Agriculture names the councillor representing Ligny-le-Châtel (not a grower himself) as official delegate of the Chablis AOC. The "Chablis men of Chablis" consider this a slap in the face.

1973. Two federations of producers come into direct confrontation. The Ministry of Agriculture proceeds to revise the defined area and entrusts Bernard Gèze, a professor of agro-geology, with the task of "identifying and defining the natural conditions of the surrounding area favourable for growing vines in the Chablis region". At last!

1976. Following the experts' report, the INAO proposes to define an extension of 148 hectares (i.e. an increase of 30 per cent) in the *Premiers Crus*, 861 hectares in the Chablis AOC, and recognizes a production area of 1,562 hectares for the Petit-Chablis. In discussion of the best vine-growing land the reference to Kimmeridgian is replaced by "marl and limestone with *Exogyra virgula*", and in sections dealing with the other areas it disappears completely. This new arrangement brings about a storm in the Chablis wineglasses. Moreover, according to some people the INAO's proposals are not always in line with the conclusions of Professor Gèze, while others find that they conform to the tried and tested methods of an historic 'terroir'. The truth of the matter remains obscure.

The result of the commission's endeavours was that the total surface area remained more or less the same (to within 12 hectares) for the Chablis *Grand Cru*, Chablis *Premier Cru* and Chablis appellations. But the commission went on to make considerable readjustments within these AOCs (for example, granting an extra 161 hectares to Beine and excluding 550 hectares for Viviers). The final results may be summarized as follows (source: *Revue du vin de France*):

– 5,272 hectares classified in the Chablis, Chablis *Premier Cru* and Chablis *Grand Cru* appellations;
– 1,562 hectares classified in Petit-Chablis;
all this out of a total area of 24,283 hectares, covering the twenty communes concerned.

Within the Chablis area, the three different appellations were divided up as follows:
Chablis: 4,419 hectares;
Chablis *Premier Cru*: 742 hectares;
Chablis *Grand Cru*: 111 hectares.

As for the Petit-Chablis, its new extent of 1,562 hectares was confirmed although the area under production at the time was only 175 hectares. Reserves of land are considerable but at the same time, as we have seen, the possibilities of extending the Chablis and Chablis *Premier Cru* are also "optimistic"– providing of course that the right to carry out new planting is granted!

The distribution of the areas as fixed is indicated commune by commune in the table overleaf.

1977. The decree establishing the new delimitations is still not signed. In the face of these repeated upheavals, by which the people of Chablis are both unsettled and frustrated, the public authorities proclaim that it is necessary to

Total production area (in hectares) of the wines of Chablis Grand Cru, Chablis Premier Cru, Chablis and Petit-Chablis AOC			
Commune	Area of commune	Chablis Grand Cru Chablis Premier Cru Chablis	Petit-Chablis
Chablis	2 047	760	50
Beine	2 079	717	805
Béru	498	275	26
Chemilly-sur-Serein	1 256	72	14
Chichée	1 816	582	82
Courgis	972	411.5	8
Fleys	799	401	18
Fontenay	494	219	51
Fyé-Chablis	1 076	298	59
La Chapelle-Vaupelteigne	484	198	–
Lignorelles	1 113	134	136
Ligny-le-Châtel	2 640	34	–
Maligny	2 170	282	161
Milly-Chablis	539	213	3
Poilly-sur-Serein	1 872	88.5	50
Préhy (St-Cyr-les-Colons)	1 391	169	12
Poinchy-Chablis	484	166	–
Rameau	1 290	5	–
Villy	364	214	87
Viviers	899	43	–
Total	24 283	5 272	1 562

delay the decision still further. To be on the safe side, they block the situation by prohibiting any new plantings. Outraged protests from the growers. The Union for the Defence of the Chablis Appellation and the Federation of Chablis growers protest vehemently.

1978. February 13: a historic date! The new delimitation of the Chablis AOCs is finally established officially. Only the confirmation of the names of the *Premiers Crus* remains.

1981. For the first time, the 1980 harvest is "approved" by a committee of experts and tasters, following the system of quality control that is already practised in Bordeaux.

1985. A series of splendid harvests (apart from 1981 which fell very short) warm the hearts of the people of Chablis by several degrees on the Baumé scale. The economy is flourishing, with a good cashflow, much of it in foreign currency. Five Ministers of Agriculture have followed each other in office since 1976. But the Minister is still the Minister. Will he sign? Suspense. Not even the winds of change following in the wake of such a rapid succession of ministers has lifted the veil of secrecy shrouding the workings of the corridors and antechambers of power. None the less, on 11 July, Pierre Marquet dutifully wrote to the Minister of Agriculture, to the Secretary of State for consumer affairs (anti-fraud branch) and to the President of the Federation for the Defence of the Chablis appellation: "The experts named by the INAO have drawn up a list of names of the *climats* classified as *Premiers Crus*, and for each one have set out the origin according to the land register of the wines which can claim this classification."

1986. The publication in the *Journal Officiel* settles the question of the *Premiers Crus* once and for all. Here it is in order to clarify the situation:

Law relating to the Chablis Appellation d'Origine Contrôlée: confirmation of the list of names of the climats *classified as* Premier Cru.

Article 1: The following names of climats *or localities are classified as* Premier Cru, *in accordance with the terms of the modified decree of January 13, 1938:*
- *Mont de Milieu*
- *Montée de Tonnerre, Chapelot, Pied d'Aloue, Côte de Bréchain*
- *Fourchaume, Vaupulent, Côte de Fontenay, L'Homme Mort, Vaulorent*
- *Vaillons, Châtains, Sécher, Beugnons, Les Lys, Mélinots, Roncières,*
- *Les Epinottes*
- *Montmains, Forêt, Butteaux*
- *Côte de Léchet*
- *Beauroy, Træsmes, Côte de Savant*
- *Vau Ligneau*
- *Vau de Vey, Vaux Ragons*
- *Vaucoupin*
- *Vosgros, Vaugiraut*
- *Les Fourneaux, Morein, Côte des Près Girots*
- *Côte de Vaubarousse*
- *Berdiot*
- *Chaume de Talvat*
- *Les Landes et Verjuts*
- *Les Beauregards, Côte de Cuissy.*

Article 2: For each of the climats *or localities classified as* Premier Cru, *the following table determines the required source of the wines within the* Chablis Premier Cru *appellation area, determined at the meeting of the National Board*

The Chablis vineyards are highly fragmented: the average area of parcels in the Premiers Crus *is less than 0.3 hectares. The following pages show vineyards on the threshold of Montée de Tonnerre.* ▶

Source of wines within the Premier Cru Chablis AOC

Climat	Commune	Land Register reference and name of locality	
Mont de Milieu *	Chablis (Fyé)	P2	Mont de Milieu
	Fleys	A4	
		A4	Vallée de Chigot
Montée de Tonnerre *	Chablis (Fyé)	P2	Montée de Tonnerre
Chapelot	Chablis (Fyé)	P2	Les Chapelots
Pied d'Aloue	Chablis (Fyé)	P2	Pied d'Aloue
		P2	Sous Pied-d'Aloue
Côte de Bréchain	Chablis (Fyé)	Ru	Côte de Bréchain
Fourchaume *	La Chapelle-Vaupelteigne	Cu	Fourchaume
Vaupulent	La Chapelle-Vaupelteigne	Cu	Vau Pulan
	Chablis (Poinchy)	Nu	Les Vaupulans
	Fontenay	C2 (ex C5)	La Fourchaume
Côte de Fontenay	Fontenay	C2 (ex C5)	La Côte
		ZD (ex C3)	Dine-Chien
L'Homme Mort	Maligny	F2	L'Homme Mort
		F1	La Grande Côte
		F2	Bois Seguin
		F3	L'Ardillier
Vaulorent *	Chablis (Poinchy)	Nu	Les 4 chemins
		Nu	La Ferme couverte
		Nu	Les Couvertes
	Fontenay	C2 (ex C5)	" "
Vaillons *	Chablis	F2	Les Vaillons
		F2	Sur les Vaillons
Châtains	Chablis	F2	Les Grands Chaumes
		F2	Les Châtains
		F1	Châtains
Sécher	Chablis	F1	Sécher
Beugnons *	Chablis	F2	Les Beugnons
Les Lys *	Chablis	F1	Les Lys
		F1	Champlain
Mélinots	Chablis	F2	Les Minos
Roncières	Chablis	F2	Les Roncières
Les Epinottes	Chablis	F1	Les Epinottes
Montmains *	Chablis	E1	Les Monts Mains
Forêt *	Chablis	E2	Les Forêts
Butteaux *	Chablis	E2	Le Bout des Butteaux
		E2	Vaux Miolot
		E3	Le Milieu des Butteaux
		E3	Les Ecueillis
		E3	Vaugerlains
Côte de Léchet *	Chablis (Milly)	H	Le Château

Beauroy *	Chablis (Poinchy)	Lu	Sous Boroy
		Lu	Vallée des Vaux
		Lu	Benfer
Trœsmes *	Beine	C1	Côte de Trœsmes
		C1	Adroit de Vau Renard
Côte de Savant	Beine	B2	Côte de Savant
		ZH	Le Cotat Château
		ZH	Frouquelin
		ZH	Le Verger
Vau Ligneau (N)	Beine	AD	Vau Vigneau
		E2	Vau de Longue
		AB	Vau Girault
		E1	" "
		ZK	" "
		E1	La Forêt
		E1	Sur La Forêt
Vau de Vey (N)	Beine	D1	Vau de Vey
		D1	La Grande Chaume
		D3	" "
Vaux Ragons	Beine	D3	Vignes des Vaux Ragons
		D5	" "
Vaucoupin *	Chichée	C1	Vaucopins
		C1	Adroit de Vaucopins
		C2	" "
Vosgros	Chichée	A1	Vosgros
		A1	Adroit de Vosgros
Vaugiraut	Chichée	A1	Vaugiraut
Les Fourneaux	Fleys	A2	Les Fourneaux
Morein	Fleys	A2	Morein
Côte des Près Girots	Fleys	B2	Côte des Près Girots
		B2	La Côte
		B2	Sur la Côte
Côte de Vaubarousse (N)	Chablis (Fyé)	O2	Côte de Vaubarousse
Berdiot (N)	Chablis (Fyé)	O2	Berdiot
Chaume de Talvat (N)	Courgis	B1	Chaumes de Talvat
Les Landes et Verjuts (N)	Courgis	B2	Les Landes et Verjuts
Les Beauregards (N)	Courgis	Du	Les Beauregards
		Du	Haut des Chambres du Roi
Côte de Cuissy (N)	Courgis	Du	Côte de Cuissy
		Du	Les Corvées
		Du	Bec d'Oiseau
		Du	Vallée de Cuissy

of the INAO on January 31, 1978 and defined by the decree of February 27, 1978.

Here I would like to interrupt the legal draftsman for a moment to explain that each *climat* classified as *Premier Cru* is a combination of several localities. For example, the *climat* called Vaulorent covers the areas called "Les Quatre Chemins", "La Ferme Couverte" and "Les Couvertes"on the land register. So wines from these areas can all be called "Vaulorent", unless the grower prefers to claim only the most specific name. But if you see a *Premier Cru* label with the words "Les Couvertes", you can be sure it is a *Premier Cru* Vaulorent.

In the preceding table, an asterisk following the name of a *climat* indicates that it is one of the most celebrated, known as the"historic" *Premiers Crus*. The most recent, the product of the INAO's new dispositions, are followed by the sign (N).

Article 3 of the decree stipulates that *"For every property, the proprietor(s) may use only one and the same* climat *name to indicate the origin of the wines produced by the sum total of the different parcels of vines situated in one* climat *classified as* Premier Cru.*"*

At present, the area of *Premiers Crus* in production is divided between eight villages and two hamlets in the Chablis appellation. In order of decreasing size, they are:

Chablis (including Fyé)	253 hectares
Beine	104 hectares
Chichée	66.5 hectares
Milly-Chablis	52 hectares
La Chapelle-Vaupelteigne	37 hectares
Fleys	35 hectares
Poinchy-Chablis	35 hectares
Maligny	33 hectares
Courgis	28 hectares
Fontenay	14.5 hectares

As for the *Grands Crus*, they remain practically static, gloriously eternal. Their proportions are considerably more modest.

Vaudésir (Moutonne)	2.4 hectares
Les Clos	24.8 hectares
Blanchot	12.2 hectares
Grenouilles	9.4 hectares
Valmur	11.9 hectares
Vaudésir	12.1 hectares
Preuses	11.1 hectares
Bougros	14.3 hectares

Any endeavour to sum up all the different elements that make up the Chablis epic leaves one tempted to whine (as it were) : "What a complicated business!" And yet I have simplified it to the point of glossing over certain aspects which the real aficionado would deem essential. To draw an analogy with the art of photography, it is a question of perspective in which the focal length, aperture, angle of vision and depth of field all depend on the photographer's personal choice. The definition of the image also depends on the time of exposure and the light-sensitivity of the plate which fixes the pictures. I am aware that some people's thirst will have been more than satisfied by my investigations, just as others will be left hungering for more information.

In the seventeenth century there were approximately 640 hectares of "Chablis" under production. A century later, vineyards flourished over some 700 hectares. By the nineteenth century, they were approaching 800 hectares. Towards the end of the twentieth century, the *Grands Crus* and the *Premiers Crus* alone total nearly 800 hectares. During this period, the "Chablis" and "Petit-Chablis" appellations have spread widely over terrains whose vine-growing potential has been proved only recently. I would say that the experts have done a good job. Overall, the Ancients and the Moderns exist perfectly well together, side by side. If the "Chablis" appellation, with all that it contains, had not been codified, it would mean no more today than a dry white wine coming more or less from the southeast of the Paris basin. But today the name of Chablis indicates four levels of perfectly controlled quality:

Grands Crus
Premiers Crus
Chablis
Petit-Chablis

The first two levels represent the "historic" Chablis, on which the reputation of the name was founded when the legions of the Roman Emperor Probus planted the first vines in the time of Astérix. Traditionalists can trace these two appellations back to Chablis' most "primitive" source.

The other two levels represent progress. A better understanding of the geology of the land, the shrinking of distances, and the vignerons' skill in agronomy have contributed to a considered extension of the name of Chablis, which now practically excludes any possible misuse of the term. This has brought carefully controlled benefits for the consumer. For everyone can now find the wine to suit their pocket within a clearly defined structure.

A new architecture has restored the façade of Chablis. The renovation of historic buildings is always a delicate matter, especially when they have suffered the ravages of time and the onslaughts of outsiders. But the "Pillars of Chablis" remain standing. Today, we can justifiably describe this work as "rehabilitation". I find the overall effect generally successful, and I am happy to be able to sketch this little monument for you.

From the land to the barrel

"Dry, limpid, perfumed, lively and light".

Was it perhaps Pierre Poupon after all, and not Raymond Dumay, who first strung together this rosary of adjectives? Or is each of them simply repeating traditional local terms? No matter: we are all in agreement, and I invite both of them to join me in a glass of Chablis *Premier Cru*; a Montée de Tonnerre, for example, or some other choice vintage.

Hubrecht Duijker (pronounced Duyker), the Dutch wine writer, dispenses with verbal flourishes when expressing his enthusiasm: "A wine of extraordinary quality which, in all Burgundy, or even in the whole world, has no equal". Henri Elwing, for his part, resorts to arabesques: "It is the discovery of an exquisitely tailored aroma totally lacking in violence, and a nose of infinite elegance. It is the charm of a bouquet, and of a titillating coolness on the taste buds." In 1952, Raymond Baudoin dedicated a lengthy article to Chablis. He stressed its colour: "The wine of Chablis should be greenish-white and transparent. Yellow is to be avoided, and as a rule indicates a wine to which the producers have not given sufficient care, the result of negligent or faulty methods." As far as I know, the first great specialist to discuss this characteristic

---

◄ *The grapes have to endure a great deal before they are ready for harvesting. They need all the vigneron's loving care if they are to reach perfection.*

of Chablis wines was Jullien in 1816 (*Topographie de tous les vignobles connus*): "According to the opinion of several scholars, the yellow colour which can be seen in white wine and in old brandy indicates the presence of a more or less large quantity of tannin, which the wood of the casks imparts; but experience having proved to me that colourless white wines develop this colour in glass bottles, I firmly believe that the colour-change is not due to any one single cause, unless we are to suppose that the tannin, of which all wines retain a greater or lesser proportion, is capable of intensifying the color, or that it acts as a colourant only after a certain time. Others believe that the yellow colour might also come from the oxidation of carbon, the presence of which in this liquid is beyond doubt. Moreover, however diverse opinions may be, the white wines of Mâcon and several cantons of Burgundy, of Touraine, Anjou and many other vineyards, though extremely clear when bottled, always take on an amber colour. It has also been noted that among the wines of different *crus* kept in casks made out of the same wood, some are likely to colour, while others remain white. In support of this statement, I could cite the wines of Chablis, in the department of the Yonne, which only rarely take on an amber colour, whereas those of several neighbouring vineyards, although they have the same qualities as regards taste, almost always colour after several months."

At the time it was difficult to anticipate the phenomena associated with oxidation. If wine-drinkers were quite happy to accept colours tending towards tones of amber or even burnt topaz for sweet wines (Hungarian Tokay, Malaga, Madeira, etc.), they also developed a heightened appreciation of the qualities of brilliance, clarity and limpidity in the dry whites. As early as 1395, Philippe the Bold prohibited the use of manure on vines, accusing it (with reason) of producing wines that were yellow and rich – not exactly sought-after qualities. And over a century earlier, in 1214, Philippe-Auguste, a great wine connoisseur before his time, organized the first international wine competition. The troubadour Henri d'Andely drew poetic inspiration from this to compose a fine and encyclopaedic ballad entitled *La Bataille des Vins*. The majority of the *crus* of France are mentioned, including:

> Wine of Chablis and of Beaune,
> As pale a yellow as moonstone,
> Greener is than horn of ram,
> But other wines care not a damn!

(In my opinion, Beaune was linked to Chablis here simply for the sake of the rhyme scheme). So for over a thousand years, if we go back as far as Charles the Bald, we can find written testimony to the "whiteness" of Chablis. So why is Chablis so white? The question deserves to be asked, for it is not enough just to observe that it is so; we also need to understand why. I have posed the question to professionals both from the area and elsewhere, all of them erudite and knowledgeable. The majority refer to tradition. Even the most eminent replied: "We do not know what the colour of white wine is." Max Léglise, for example, the former director of the Oenological Centre of Burgundy in Beaune, and Professor Emile Peynaud, the high priest of contemporary oenology, both agree that they are totally ignorant as to the nature of the "colouring matter" in white wine. With regard to Chablis, Max Léglise believes that their lack of colour is the result of some ecological factor. The chalky soil produces a number of polyphenols which are particularly resistant to oxidation. On the other hand, the climate of Chablis very rarely allows the chardonnay grapes to become over-mature, and the colour of their skin changes little right up to the time when they are harvested. Soil, climate and grape thus combine to produce a rather high acidity level (never less than 4.50 grams per litre) and a low pH. Max Léglise's personal theory is that in Chablis, because of the climate and the soil, the chardonnay grape produces very little of the yellow pigments associated with chlorophyll. It is true that the same variety grown on a less chalky soil will give yellower grapes. It has also been proved that whatever the terrain the chardonnay will turn colour only under intense heat. Among white wine-growing areas there is no soil more chalky than that of Chablis nor any climate harsher than that of the Serein. This is why Chablis is an albino among wines.

This is also the opinion of Professor Emile Peynaud, who displays the same scientific modesty as his eminent colleague: "We do not know what the colour of white wine is." For both of them the only possible comparison is with the "blanc de blancs" wines of the hills of Champagne. These share similar ecological conditions, with a few very slight differences: chardonnay stock, chalky soil and cool temperatures. Emile Peynaud is tempted to say that in Chablis the chardonnay never ripens completely. Vinification, with rapid pressing and no maceration, accentuates even further the must's resistance to taking on colour. It appears that the yellow is imparted by xanthophyll pigments, which are closely related to chlorophyll, although we are not yet able to analyse their interaction with any certainty.

I have interpreted these opinions rather freely to conclude that, if the wine of Chablis is a greenish-white rather than a yellowy-white, it is because the grapes have more chlorophyll than xanthophyll, and that this is the result of climatic conditions peculiar to Chablis. In other words, this *chef d'œuvre* can exist only at the very extremity of nature's creation, for nowhere else does the chardonnay grape have to endure conditions of such sublime suffering. Perhaps this is why Chablis has become so revered !

Let us return for a moment to Jullien in order to corroborate his remark on ageing in the cask. It is quite clear that wines or spirits change colour on contact with new wood, so much so that chips of oak or rowan-wood are used to line the bottom of casks in Armagnac or Cognac. Today in Chablis only the *Grands Crus* and a few *Premiers Crus* can enjoy the extravagant luxury of ageing in wood. And as wines which are whiter-than-white are undeniably

in fashion, keeping them in the vat is the best precaution against oxidation. In a great wine a certain slight yellowing may be tolerated at a pinch. This is the case with Meursault and Montrachet, for example. But curiously enough, yellow wines are generally suspected of being sweet. Professor Emile Peynaud once observed this to me and, as usual, he is right. He himself was surprised when he tasted a sample of pale Sauternes. A wine-taster needs to be able to rely on all his senses. If the eye is deceived at the outset, the fragile structure on which judgement depends is in danger of collapse. Peynaud concludes: "We should be able to tell by the eye alone whether a wine is dry or sweet." Only a true expert with a great deal of experience would venture to make such a statement!

78

Chablis wines aged in wood, which are becoming increasingly rare, may therefore vary in colour. It is their way of showing their distinction; but the initial greenness will always remain as the wine turns to a green-gold. The others require more patience. They need time to digest their acidity and to assimilate it into a perfect whole. The wines of Chablis finish maturing in the bottle, just as apples or pears gathered just before the wasps arrive finish ripening on the shelf, where they develop their subtlest flavour. I have never liked the word "ageing" in the context of wines. For me it always has inescapable overtones of infirmity and loss of vigour. I much prefer the term *affinage* for this last step in a wine's journey towards perfection. There are four stages in the development of the finished product: maturity of the grape, vinification, ageing in the vat or the cask, and time in the bottle. Never underestimate the importance of this latter – provided that it is not used as an excuse for pretentiousness. I know many tasters, professionals and amateurs, for whom the time for opening a bottle is never right. In the Chartrons, the wine trading district of Bordeaux, they are legion. There are some in Chablis, too. Their logic is unassaible, and takes two forms:

First hypothesis: it is a pity to drink it so soon. It is too young and will benefit from ageing.

Second hypothesis: it is rather too late to drink it. It is already declining. Oh, what a shame.

In short, the moment is never right. This sort of showing off makes me despair. Certain producers make it a point of honour to affect such airs. In an attempt to rationalize the drinking of Chablis, I would say that there should be an interval of one to two years between each of the four appellations before uncorking. Taking the 1988 harvest as an example, the best possible time for drinking it will be: for Petit-Chablis, in 1989-90; for Chablis, in 1990-91; for Chablis *Premier Cru*, in 1991-3; for Chablis *Grand Cru*, in 1993-5.

Of course this is not a hard and fast rule. The intrinsic quality of the vintage can play a decisive role. In great years, the *Grands* and *Premiers Crus* have a longer lifespan in front of them. In 1952, in the *Revue du vin de France*, Raymond Baudoin, whom I have already quoted, wrote: "The wines of Chablis, if they are good vintages, can obviously age; there are some 1921 wines still to be found in perfect condition. But that was an exceptional year. Only rarely do Chablis wines live longer than twenty years. On the contrary, we believe that they are wines to be drunk early on, and like beautiful women, should be enjoyed in their youth."

Personally, I thoroughly disagree with the last statement as regards both fine Chablis wines and beautiful women. In either sphere, it is unwise to be so categorical. But each to his own tastes and fantasies! If Petit-Chablis is perfecly suited to carafes and wine bars, and can be drunk from the January following the harvest, the other wines of the appellation largely deserve to be aged in the bottle.

Just as there are time lapses to be observed between each level of the Chablis designations, so the most careful drinkers will drink Chablis at a temperature which increases with the quality of the wine. It is best to drink Petit-Chablis at 5-6 °C (41-43 °F), Chablis at 6-7 °C (43-45 °F), *Premiers Crus* at 7-8 °C (45-46 °F) and the *Grands Crus* at 8-9 °C (46-48 °F). Too intense a cold deadens the taste buds, and it is a waste to serve a Vaudésir excessively chilled. When you offer a good Chablis to your friends, or when you drink it in a restaurant, make sure that the glasses are not too full, as the wine quickly warms up to the ambient temperature. If the wine waiter fills your glass to only a third of its capacity, and rushes to maintain this level after every mouthful, do not take it as a display of excessive zeal. He is right, and he has your pleasure at heart, for he is ensuring a near-constant temperature and degree of air-contact. The golden rule can be summed up as: "Little and often".

What is the right glass for Chablis? It is local custom to use a tulip-shaped wineglass, slightly narrowing at the mouth, and I would not disagree with this. In any event, it is best to avoid glasses that are too elaborate or pretentious, or made of cut-glass, or, even worse, coloured glass. Avoid also glasses which are too large, in which you lose your nose every time you take a sip. In my opinion, the best possible glass is that used by professional tasters and adopted in 1970 by the European Technical Commission. It is also the standard French INAO tasting glass, and is not difficult to obtain in Britain. Its dimensions are shown here. The glass should never be filled above its widest diameter. If you have the good fortune to inherit an old bottle of Fourchaume left forgotten in your great-uncle's cellar, take time to drink it slowly after dinner, after gently cooling it in a bucket of water containing no ice. And taste it in a brandy glass with your eyes closed. Satisfaction guaranteed.

If there are seven *Grands Crus*, like Snow White's dwarfs, the Chablis *Premiers Crus* now number forty. It is practically impossible to order them into a natural hierarchy. Depending on whether you like firmness or delicacy you will prefer a Montée de Tonnerre or a Mont de Milieu, and so on. On the other hand, every *climat* does not react in the same way in any given year. You can find a 1982 Vaucoupin which is much better than a Vaillons of the same year, and vice versa in 1983. Much also depends on the personal style of the vintner himself. From experience, I rely on a combination of the largest number of authoritative opinions. This is why I have gathered together in one table as many published opinions as I could find. I should point out that their authors only cite the appellations in their broadest sense, without going into details of the *climats* each contains. I do not claim that

81

Grands Crus

Albert Pic	Nicolas	P. Galet	J.-F. Bazin	P. Poupon	H. Johnson
Blanchot	Vaudésir	Vaudésir	Blanchot	Vaudésir	Blanchots
Les Clos	Valmur	Les Clos	Bougros	Preuses	Bougros
Valmur	Grenouille	Valmur	Les Clos	Les Clos	Les Clos
Grenouille	Les Clos	Grenouilles	Grenouilles	Grenouilles	Grenouilles
Vaudésir	Blanchot	Bougros	Preuses	Bougros	Preuses
	Preuse	Preuse	Valmur	Valmur	Valmur
		Blanchot	Vaudésir	Blanchots	Vaudésir
			(In order of preference)		(In order of preference)

A. Lichine	R. George	W. Fèvre	R. Dumay	Consensus
Les Clos	Blanchot	Blanchots	Vaudésir	**Vaudésir**
Vaudésir	Preuses	Bougros	Preuses	**Les Clos**
Les Preuses	Bougros	Les Clos	Les Clos	**Preuses**
Valmur	Grenouilles	Grenouilles	Grenouilles	**Grenouilles**
Blanchot	Valmur	Preuses	Bougros	**Valmur**
Grenouilles	Vaudésir	Valmur	Valmur	**Blanchot**
Bougros	Les Clos	Vaudésir	Blanchots	**Bougros**
		(In order of preference)		

Premiers Crus
(The first three columns distinguish between 1st and 2nd groups)

Albert Pic	Nicolas	P. Galet	J.-F. Bazin	P. Poupon	H. Johnson
Mont de Milieu	Bougros	Mont de Milieu	Fourchaume	Mont de Milieu	Fourchaume
Chapelot	Vaulorent	Chapelots	Montée de Tonnerre	Montée de Tonnerre	Montée de Tonnerre
Montée de Tonnerre	Fourchaume	Montée de Tonnerre	Mont de Milieu	Fourchaume	Monts de Milieu
Preuses	Chapelot	Fourchaume	Vaucoupin	Vaillons	Vaucoupin
Bougros	Mont de Milieu	Vaulorent	Côte de Fontenay	Montmains	Les Fourneaux
Fourchaume	Montée de Tonnerre		L'Homme Mort	Mélinots	Beauroy
Vaulorent	Pied d'Aloue		Vaillons	Côte de Léchet	Côte de Léchet
———	———	———	Montmains	Beauroy	Vaillons
Forêt	Vaillon	Forêt	Côte de Léchet	Vaucoupin	Mélinots
Montmain	Montmains	Montmain	Forêt	Vosgros	Montmains
Beugnon	Séchet	Beugnon	Les Lys	Les Fourneaux	Vogros
Vaillons	Beugnon	Vaillons	Beugnons		Vaudevey
Mélinots	Forêt	Mélinots	Beauroy		
Roncières	Mélinots	Roncières	Trœsmes		
Les Lys	Roncières	Les Lys	Vaulorent		
Séchet	Les Lys	Séchet	Vosgros		
Les Epinottes		Epinotte	Vaugiraut		
Vaucoupin		Vaucoupin	Butteaux		
Côte de Léchet		Côte de Léchet			
Beauroy		Beauroy			
Trœsmes		Trœsmes			
Côte de Fontenay		Côte de Fontenay			

A. Lichine	R. George	W. Fèvre	R. Dumay	General classification of the twelve Chablis Premiers Crus
Vaulorent	Fourchaume	Montée de Tonnerre	Beauroy	**Fourchaume**
Fourchaume	Montée de Tonnerre	Fourchaume	Côte de Léchet	**Montée de Tonnerre**
Montée de Tonnerre	Mont de Milieu	Vaulorent	Forêt	**Mont de Milieu**
Mont de Milieu	Vaucoupin	Mont de Milieu	Fourchaume	**Vaulorent**
Vaillons	Les Fourneaux	Vaucoupin	Mélinot	**Chapelots**
Montmains	Beauroy	Côte de Fontenay	Mont de Milieu	**Montmains**
Forêt	Côte de Léchet	L'Homme Mort	Montée de Tonnerre	**Vaillons**
	Vaillons	Vaillons	Montmains	**Beugnons**
	Mélinots	Côte de Léchet	Vaillons	**Forêt**
	Montmains	Montmains	Vaucoupin	**Vaucoupin**
	Vosgros	Les Lys	Vaugiraut	**Côte de Léchet**
		Forêt	Vosgros	**Trœsmes**
		Beugnons	(In order of	
		Boroy	preference)	
		Trœsmes		
		Vosgros		
		Vaugiraut		
		Butteaux		

this is the only approach, nor that it should be accepted. But it at least has the merit of existing, and may serve as a guideline for the neophyte. It would be possible to discuss these lists *ad infinitum*. I shall limit my observations to a few comments: In the *Grands Crus*, Preuses and Bougros are the latecomers to this ultra-select club. Subtle distinctions should be made within each *cru*. Moutonne, which is not mentioned in the classification, corresponds to the best part of Vaudésir. If Bougros is on the boundary, the Pointe des Bougros is an excellent microclimate. Blanchot is capable of producing superb bottles, etc. In the *Premiers Crus*, it is interesting to compare the order of this list with the "historic" *Premiers Crus* favoured by William Fèvre:

	Historic Premiers Crus	Our classification
1st group	Mont de Milieu	Fourchaume
	Montée de Tonnerre	Montée de Tonnerre
	Fourchaume	Mont de Milieu
	Vaulorent	Vaulorent
2nd group	Vaillons	Chapelot
	Beugnons	Montmains
	Les Lys	Vaillons
	Montmains	Beugnons
	Forêt	Forêt
3rd group	Butteaux	Vaucoupin
	Côte de Léchet	Côte de Léchet
	Beauroy	Trœsmes
	Trœsmes	Butteaux
	Vaucoupin	Beauroy

There is no doubt about the first three: they have pride of place, and indeed I have drunk Fourchaumes which have been infinitely superior to some *Grands Crus*. There is parity within the second group, though. I have inserted Chapelot instead of Les Lys. It is a little-used *climat* name, like its neighbour Pied-d'Aloue, and both are more or less assimilated into Montée de Tonnerre, of which they are a continuation towards the bottom of the valley of the Serein. In the same way, very remarkable *crus* such as L'Homme Mort or Vaupulent, or even Côte de Fontenay, are also neighbours of Fourchaume and share similar qualities, but are little known to the public. There is in any case, a preponderance among the leading names of *crus* from the right bank. Nevertheless, the fame of certain *Premiers Crus* on the left bank is far from eclipsed: Montmains, Vaillons, Beugnons, Côte de Léchet, Les Lys and Beauroy are capable of being exceptional. And as for the rest, it should not be forgotten that they too are *Premiers Crus*, though many remain unrecognized or unknown. They all warrant being discovered, whatever their *finage*.

At that very moment, a child of tender age
Asked me the question: what is a *finage*?

"This word, whose use is rather archaic, means almost the same thing as the word *village*. In the language of vignerons, it means primarily the land of the village rather than the village itself. So its meaning is more cognate with the word *terroir*" (Pierre Poupon and Sylvain Pitiot, *Atlas des grands vignobles de Bourgogne*, Ed. Jacques Legrand, Paris, 1985). Formerly, the *finage* was "the extent of the area over which a lord or a town had the right of jurisdiction" (P. Larousse). Today, *finage* is used almost exclusively in a viticultural sense. It does not have quite the same meaning as the word *village* because originally it was used to designate the extent of the lands dependent on a village. *Finage* anticipates the commune. Most of the time, the land of the *finage* covers the extent of a parish comprising several villages surrounding one church. "I am a large tithe-owner of the *finage*, and as priest I receive about fifteen hundred livres; five hundred francs are enough for the upkeep of my house. The rest ought not to go out of my parish, which is poor," said the priest of Courgis in about 1750 (Rétif de La Bretonne, op. cit.).

Today in the Chablis area, the *finage* means all the good land under vines within the confines of the communal limits. Thus, the *Premiers Crus* Fourchaume and Vaupulent belong to the *finage* of La Chapelle-Vaupelteigne. I have noted a certain tendency in some people to use the terms *finage* and *climat* indiscriminately. In order to protect the true meaning of the words, we should try not to confuse them. Although the word *finage* (which was written *finaige* in the thirteenth century) comes from the Latin *finis*, meaning confines, limits or territory, the modern derivation of this word has the added implication of quality, thus refining our knowledge of the finite.

The local dialect is disappearing here, as everywhere else in France, and is now practically confined to folk-songs. It is more a way of speaking than a separate language with deep etymological roots, and it encapsulates the accent of the area in its phonetic spelling. Rétif de La Bretonne gives us a number of delightful examples. They find a rough equivalent in British dialects, for example:

"*Père Dulis (to his workers).* And the vines, lads?
A vigneron. Ah, to be sure, boss. 'Tis foin they are! Dur buds are as big as yer tumb. And such grapes, begorrah! 'Twill be a foin harvest even if dur remayns only hahf of what dair is now."

More recently, in the collection entitled *Poésie auxerroise et chansons vigneronnes* (1927), there appeared a song entitled "The Vigneron's Griefs". Taking an equally sturdy British dialect for translation, the last verse would sound something like this:

> Bah gumm! Us tea is dee-lec-table,
> Wi' beans and spuds piled 'igh ont'table;
> There's thick pea soup, and Ma's lamb stew;
> 'Ts that good we licks us fingers too!
> An' in yon jug a pint o'wollop
> What's just the job for us beef collop.
> And there in t'grate, the logs burn breet
> As keeps us warm all through the neet.

Further renderings of the Icaune dialect (the inhabitants of the Yonne are called Icaunes) can be found at the end of this book, in a short anthology of Chablis poetry. I have included them there to bring us closer to the land and its people. The living conditions of the vignerons have changed considerably for the better since the beginning of this century. It can be said without exaggeration, however, that at the end of the nineteenth century little had changed since the Middle Ages. With their land split up into little parcels and small family estates , most people lived barely at subsistance level. The system under which they existed was simple: at the bottom of the hill, vegetables, poultry, pigs; halfway up, vines and a few cereals; and at the top, coppices and more livestock. And all this spread out over plots of, on average, not more than two or three hectares per family. This explains the Chablis growers' life of poverty, though it does not convey the harshness of their existence. But by its very endurance this firmly rooted peasantry was to form the foundation of local society. So much so that today it is still the growers who as it were rule the roost. Between the last quarter of the nineteenth century and the first quarter of the twentieth, that is over about two generations, the local bourgeoisie was obliged to quit the field to all intents and purposes because it had not been able to look after its own interests, whereas the people working the land continued to do so in the face of all adversity. As my purpose here

Since the spread of mechanization and its remarkable progress, work in the vineyards has become more efficient, even on steep slopes and difficult terrain. From planting to trimming and harvesting, the vigneron is now able to work rapidly and effectively.

is not to present a sociological thesis, I will conclude by quoting Gérald Jack Gilbank: "And so a cycle came full circle. The Chablis estates were taken over at a time when they were the perquisite of a local bourgeoisie originating from the vineyards and made rich by business in wine. But because these estates were not split up among people from outside and were readjusted in every generation by intermarriages, which allowed nothing to fall into the hands of outsiders, they came through a whole century and its crises to emerge today apparently intact. But at the same time as they were maintaining their vineyards, these family proprietors who were building their own future on the profits of the wine business were also producing heirs for whom the milieu of 'principal town of the canton' would become too restrictive. The affluent bourgeois estates of the beginning of the nineteenth century thus became drained of their substance, were perhaps badly administered from afar, and crumbled at a time when there was not one single sign to justify any hope of the vineyards' coming into their own again."

The first signs of the rebirth of hope in Chablis came with the foundation of the *coopérative* in 1923. It was one of the very first in France, pre-dating the development of the viticultural co-operative movement of the thirties following the 1929 economic crisis. A crisis had already had Chablis in its grip for ten years. So the *coopérative* called La Chablisienne is also a "child of

▲ *Certain jobs are still done by hand – pruning, for example, and afterwards, "training down", being carried out here. The hooked pliers used for tying the branch are known as "la baissette".* ▶

88

sorrow". In 1919, a quarter-cask of wine could find no takers at 550 francs. Three years later it would remain unsold at prices that had dropped by fifty per cent. Three men together decided to do something about it. The moving spirit of this triumvirate was Balitran, the priest of Poinchy, who was assisted by Fernand Pinsot, an official in public administration, and a retired teacher by the name of Persenoud. To begin with they helped the small producers to sell their wines directly in the places where the wine was drunk. At that time local wine merchants had a near monopoly on wine purchases and had no scruples about hammering prices down or postponing their orders from month to month in order to be able finally to buy an entire harvest against settlement of accounts opened with the grocer or the butcher. It was another "unholy war"which saw the priest Balitran set out on a crusade against the infidels of the local wine trade who were prostituting the name of Chablis. The result was a bloody schism between the growers and the merchants. Many producers saw their final illusions fade away together with their last sou, but fifty or so of them took a liking to this idea of solidarity, which was new to them. Today, La Chablisienne is a *coopérative* efficient in vinification, blending and marketing; a fuller description can be found in the second part of this book. In its early beginnings and up to the Second World War, it revolutionized the mentality and economic customs of the people of Chablis.

Another revolution came with the advent of the tractor, which overturned viticulture in Chablis as it did the Kimmeridgian clay. All at once, the slopes seemed less steep and the estates seemed to have shrunk to the size of a pocket handkerchief. This change took place in the fifties. These mobile steam-horses replaced animal-drawn equipment or motorized winches. As everywhere in France, a generation found that two men could do in five days what three or four men would have managed in a seven-day week, and moreover that the tractor did not whinny for food or because it felt cold. Emboldered by these new methods of locomotion and cultivation, the vignerons now pioneered the conquest of new lands. Terrain once thought to be inaccessible and hardly viable was explored, tested and exploited. Mechanization spread throughout the area and the younger generation took heart again. Heavy equipment had arrived in Chablis. For centuries, "porters" had carried back up on their backs the precious limestone brought down the slopes by erosion. Bulldozers were now put to the task. For them it was child's play. Sometimes, however, they overstepped the bounds of duty, shamelessly carting away loads of earth, unconcerned by distances and provoking intense concern among the traditional growers. Feelings ran high. Headlines in the most outspoken local

◄ *Modernization flies to the aid of the vignerons at spraying time.*

Some viticulturalists, meanwhile, remain fervently committed to traditional harvesting methods. ►

newspapers screamed that they were having "the ground cut from under their feet". And yet by and large the vineyards were rejuvenated. However glorious the Middle Ages may have been for Chablis, they were finally left behind. The modernization which seized Chablis body and soul brought about its salvation. Over the course of a thousand years, the men of Chablis have blended tradition with practice – a combination which may ultimately be a form of resignation. Between 1955 and 1975 (a period which saw changes as far-ranging as those of the Jurassic era), a new wine-producing age and a new viticultural era had dawned in Chablis. And a successful one.

Now the only variety grown in Chablis is the pinot chardonnay, now known almost universally simply as chardonnay, though it is still beaunois to those who know it intimately. Before the phylloxera crisis, a number of more or less prolific and common (in both senses) varieties were to be found in Chablis, such as the aligoté, sacy, melon, etc. Then came the apocalypse, the Last Judgement of the vines. All were exterminated by the Devil's little insect, but the chardonnay rose again, the last of the righteous. When phylloxera set in, Chablis had approximately 675 hectares of vines, of which 125 were on *Premier Cru* land. Gradually the chardonnay found its place in the sun again, grafted progressively onto American rootstock. Today it reigns supreme over the Chablis vineyards. The study of grape varieties is called ampelography. Formerly – over a century ago – everybody used to get into a muddle because the same varieties had different names from region to region. The chardonnay, for example, had no fewer than thirty synonyms! If three vignerons were to meet up to talk shop, a man from Champagne would say that he cultivated the *epinette*, the man from the Jura would reply with the *petit chatey* and the man from Touraine knew only the *arnaison*. And yet all three men would be discussing the same variety.

It is from the "fourth leafing" that grapes have the right to their *appellation d'origine*. Such is the case in the majority of AOC vineyards. There is nothing special about the cultivation cycle. Hoeing has now been replaced by herbicides. Pruning goes on all through winter right up to the month of March. The Double Guyot system of pruning is still practised, leaving twenty or so buds. It is followed by "training down", which consists of tying the main branch to a wire lower down to keep it as close as possible to the ground during the struggle against April and May frosts. Budding generally takes place very quickly, in a virtual explosion of green. At the beginning of May the vines still appear to be dormant, but two weeks later they are covered in tender young growth: "At Whitsuntide, you can see the vines coming into leaf from one hill to the next." Once the risk of frost is over, the vines are treated against their

---

Enamelled steel vats are increasingly replacing wooden casks. In the foreground is an earth filter of the Kieselguhr type. ▶

natural enemies, cryptogamic diseases or insect pests and unwanted shoots are trimmed regularly. As in the Bordeaux region, harvesting will take place a hundred days after flowering, that is on about October 5. The "ban des vendanges", a survival of the *ancien régime*, is announced by a decree from the *préfecture*. As soon as they are gathered, the grapes are taken to the press and crushed very quickly, the skins never being allowed to macerate in the must. The latter is usually fermented in vats. Traditionalists put it into cask and some *Grands* and *Premiers Crus* still use new wood. After effervescing for a few days, the must changes into a cloudy, slightly sparkling sweet wine. This is the new unfermented wine, called in French the "vin bourru".

Up to the Second World War, this new wine used to be served by the glass in the majority of bars and restaurants in Paris. Today its sale is prohibited, but it remains a tradition in Chablis, and every year when the time comes families and friends gather together to taste it. Its alcohol content is about 11°. It still needs another 1.5° before it will be a fully-fledged Chablis. It is said to have many health-giving qualities: it is certainly very effective for cleansing the blood!

Controlled chaptalization is standard practice. The quantities of sugar used are more or less fixed, but depend on the vintage. The best-equipped cellars use cooling equipment to accelerate the precipitation of tartar crystals and lees. You can still find producers who are faithful to the old ways and to the tradition of ageing the wine in the traditional local casks of 132 litres, but there are at least as many others in favour of the standard-size barrel. In 1984, Sotheby's published an excellent work on Chablis by Rosemary George. She was particularly interested in the question of ageing, and the results of her research may be summarized as follows.

Does ageing wine in wood improve it, or is it detrimental to quality? The modern school claims to be allergic to wood and strives for a youthful, fresh style. To this end, firms such as J. Moreau et Fils prefer the stainless steel vat to all other wine-making vessels. Certain firms even store their wines in nitrogen to prevent any risk of oxidation. At the other extreme are men such as William Fèvre. In 1979, he constructed a new cellar for the express purpose of housing new wooden casks. All his wines spend four to five months in new oak. He thinks that the natural aromas of the wine develop better in casks than in vats, and the resulting oxidation, though imperceptible, plays a role in bringing them out. Moreover, new wood adds a complementary touch of tannin, and if the wine remains long enough in the barrel, clarification will take place through a natural settling of the lees, making brutal filtration unnecessary.

Somewhere between these two positions is Michel Laroche. His firm has all the latest wine-making equipment but, like Gérard Vullien of Long Depaquit, he thinks that the *Grands Crus* and perhaps certain *Premiers Crus* benefit from spending a certain amount of time in wood. Here I find myself in agreement

98

There are still many traditionalists who swear by the virtues of oak casks. Above: Monsieur Dauvissat among his casks. Below: part of Monsieur Fèvre's cellars.

99

with Hugh Johnson and the late Alexis Lichine. The best *crus* of Chablis only reach their full aromatic potential when matured in casks of new oak.

Another school, to which a few small producers subscribe, remains faithful to the good old casks, using the same ones over several generations. They claim that new oak makes the wines far too tannic. François Raveneau and René Dauvissat, attached as they are to wood, do not renew their casks too often. They are perhaps right. Whatever the case, their matured wines are more often than not quite remarkable.

The connoisseur should try out for himself the individual styles which are the result of each different method. Today there is a Chablis for all tastes – and for nearly every pocket. So it is up to each individual to find the wine that suits him. While installing modern vats is an expensive investment, the purchase and upkeep of a stock of casks is even more costly in relation to the volume of the wine they contain. There is also always a certain amount of loss through evaporation from wine kept in wood, whereas a stainless steel vat always gives back the quantity it started out with. The amount of Chablis which disappears into thin air – known as the "angels' share" – is always a matter of poignant regret.

To be complete, this panorama of Chablis should really include a discussion of the age of the vines. This is a matter of fierce controversy, however. As may be imagined, the modern trend is to seek rapid returns on the capital invested in a vineyard. A young vine yields good quality from its fifth year. At ten years it reaches its peak, and its life expectancy is only some fifteen years. Then it is replaced. I do not think that it is misplaced sentimentality to like wines from old vine-stock, however. Obviously, the yields per hectare also decline with age. But the Blanchots of Laroche, which have seen nearly forty springs, are, in my humble opinion, among the most sublime Chablis which can be tasted. I should emphasize, of course, that I am talking here of the age of the vines, not of the wine.

In former days a plantation was considered to have a lifespan of half a century or more. Two or three generations could follow one another, and grandfather would come along in his cart to watch his grandson pruning "his" beaunois. Now the rhythm of renewing stock has quickened pace and gained considerable and apparently unstoppable momentum. That is progress for you. It cannot be reversed. A Chablis man may not yet have travelled to the moon, but he nevertheless consults it less than he used to when wondering what the weather is going to do. In two or three years, the growers of Chablis will have access to the most up-to-date meteorological information via teletext. By satellite, of course. But this does not stop them from celebrating the festival of Saint-Vincent, even though it has now become a "secular" festival. In the following chapter we shall see how the people of Chablis continue to live out their traditions, not as historic rituals, nor out of nostalgia for the

past, but as a living heritage being turned to account. The balance of a great wine hangs on this hinge, opening the door from yesterday on to today.

The day before yesterday, the knife-grinder used to go round the streets of Chablis every Tuesday. Today it is cheaper to buy a new knife rather than have it sharpened.

The day before yesterday, similarly, the travelling press went round from family to family at harvest-time. Now it is the harvest which goes to the press. Its programme is transistorized. Forty harvesters have now been replaced by one mobile machine, and secateurs are destined to become museum pieces. In a short time (one or two centuries, if history permits), computerized ethnologists will be using oral records to explain how grape secateurs were used. Was the day before yesterday a better time? Surely not. It was a different time.

▲ *In former days the travelling press went round from family to family at harvest time.*

Gastronomy, local traditions – and the bill, please!

"Dry, limpid, perfumed, lively and light".

Words evoke ideas which often outstrip their meaning. Sound plays an important part in the picture each word conjures up. Nothing smoother than the word "smooth", for example. Professor Roman Jakobson wrote a superb essay on this subject. But there are times when, to be sure of communicating our precise meaning, we need to examine the full significance of the language, especially when it is being used to describe a precise idea.

I should therefore like to quote from the *Dictionnaire du vin* (Féret et Fils, Bordeaux, 1962):

Dry: A white wine is said to be dry when it contains no residual sugars.

Limpidity: A condition of a clear, transparent, brilliant wine, in which all matters in suspension have fallen to the bottom of the vessel which contains it, forming lees. It is not possible to establish a scale for the limpidity of wines, because an absolute definition of the limpidity of a liquid cannot be given, since the density of any opacity and the sensitivity with which it is perceived depend on the way it is viewed. The condition of limpidity is an entirely relative notion.

Perfume: See *Aroma, Bouquet* and *Fruit*.

◄ *The "moveable feast" of Saint-Vincent takes place in a different commune every year. It allows everyone to give free rein to their feelings in the purest Dionysiac tradition.*

Aroma: According to Norbert Got, in his work *La Dégustation des vins*, 'the aroma corresponds to what some also call the nose of the fruit, the primary bouquet or the original bouquet. This comes from the grape. Unlike the bouquet, the aroma diminishes with age, and may be said to reach its peak in the first year. Its freshness and fullness fade with time.' Formerly, the word perfume was used particularly for white wines, bouquet or nose being used for red wines and aroma for spirits.

Bouquet: The frank, agreeable odour of a wine, called the bouquet, constitutes the distinctive character of fine wines. The olfactory analysis through which we may perceive the splendours of each *cru* can be broken down into three different sensations on the nose:

– The primary bouquet (that is the original bouquet coming specifically from the grape) ;

– The secondary bouquet, which develops during the fermentation process; this perfume is supplied by the yeasts, and results particularly from the formation of superior alcohols and their derivatives, the aldehydes and esters;

– The final tertiary bouquet which develops with maturity and which accordingly, develops during ageing.

Fruity: Is used for a wine which recalls the taste of fresh grapes to the palate. The fruity taste is greatly valued in new wines. This characteristic disappears with age.

Lively: A lively wine penetrates right to the back of the palate, making a strong impression without offering any acid or alcoholic flavour. Liveliness is generally characterized by a bright shining colour.

Light: Is used of a wine which has little colour, body or vinosity [flavour and strength] but in which the constituent elements are correctly balanced. Such wine can often be very pleasant."

With this extract from the dictionary we may all imbibe some of the learning of Chablis. In one of Hergé's famous Tintin books, *Destination Moon*, the young reporter's chum, Captain Haddock, takes a bottle of his favourite tipple from a false bookcase: "Let us broach the first volume", he says ironically. And after the first glassful, he exclaims: "Ah! Already I feel better informed!" This little pantomime makes me think of Boileau, who as we have already mentioned was the proprietor of a vineyard not far from Chablis:

> One is learned when one knows how to drink,
> The man who does not know how to drink knows nothing.

Wines are like good politics: being able to, knowing how to and having the will to are closely linked. It follows that any responsible citizen should know how to drink Chablis. Apart from the right temperature and shape of glass, it should also be married with the right food, just as, in days of old, intermediaries of princely crowns endeavoured to negotiate judicious marriages of heart and

state. The first course which inevitably springs to mind when we speak of Chablis is oysters, a liaison which, as we have already seen, goes way back in time. If you were to go to the Brasserie Lipp to order a bottle of Côte de Léchet with five dozen (enough for two, given their size) *Exogyra virgula*, you would be correct in geological terms, though the chances of being able to do this are now small. Yet we have already seen how the epicurean Pierre-Antoine-Augustin de Piis sang the praises of the combination of Chablis wine and oysters. And before him, F. de Courcy wrote the following lines:

> With fine fresh oysters for my fare
> Good Chablis wine is pure delight!
> Both fame and fortune I'd forswear
> To succumb to this wine so bright
> With fine fresh oysters for my fare!

▲ *"The wine of Chablis is dry, fresh and light, with a fine bouquet "; its marriage with seafoods is pure connubial bliss, but it also has much wider gastronomic possibilities.*

105

The modern encyclopaedists of wine go one better: "A beautiful pale yellow colour with hints of green, the wine of Chablis is dry, fresh and light, with a fine bouquet; it goes marvellously well with fish, shellfish, snails" (*Dictionnaire du vin*). In short, it would seem that Chablis is destined to be wedded with seafood in some eternal idyll. In fact shellfish and crustaceans really are the best accompaniment to Chablis. It is as if there were a sort of affinity between the greenish-whiteness of the oyster and the colour of the wine.

But let us begin at the beginning. A Petit-Chablis or a young Chablis is one of the best possible bases for making the aperitif "kir". I knew Canon Kir towards the end of his life, when he was still the oldest member of the National Assembly. He was kind enough to give me an audience several times. One day, I risked teasing him about his "invention". He winked slyly at me: "I have invented nothing. I have only helped to make something better known. It is as good as any other way of going down in history. And I hope that the Good Lord will not hold it against me. We shall see later on!" Like Vespasian, Silhouette and Poubelle before it, Kir has entered the French language in its own right. In order to avoid being too boringly conventional, I am in favour of varying the fruits used in making kir. It is possible, after all, to tire of blackcurrant. We should surely allow ourselves the pleasure of discovering Petit-Chablis with raspberry, strawberry, cherry brandy, or even lemon. Yes, you may be surprised by *Chablicitron*, the super-invigorating aperitif, I predict, of the year 2000.

The wine of Chablis is also a wine for (gourmet) cooking. Its natural acidity, fully enhanced by its esters and other volatile constituents, is ideal for enriching light, savoury sauces. This book is not meant to be a collection of recipes, but as an example here are two dishes which form part of the Chablis tradition and which are quite delicious. The first is snails with Chablis. In winter the Chablis area is home to large numbers of hibernating snails. These burrow into the earth at the onset of winter, having eaten their way steadily through the tender leaves of the chardonnay vine all through the summer. Their sleep is not always undisturbed. Formerly, the vignerons who unearthed them used to eat them raw with salt, or simply grilled over an open fire. Today, if you are fortunate enough to have a few of these delicious snails you might prefer to try the following recipe, taken from that wonderful book *Le Goût de la France* (Flammarion, 1985): "For 4 people, take 4 dozen snails, 2 large glasses of Chablis, 2 large glasses of stock, 1 large *bouquet garni*, 2 shallots, 1 clove of garlic, sea-salt, freshly ground pepper, 1 small glass of brandy, 1 cupful of fresh breadcrumbs. To make the snail butter, take 12 ounces (350 g) of butter, 1 clove of garlic, 2 shallots, 2 table-spoonsful of

Visitors always receive a warm welcome at Odile and Michel Soulié's shop in Chablis, which sells the finest andouillette *and a judicious selection of local wines.* ▶

chopped parsley, salt and pepper. The basic preparation for snails is always the same. They must be thoroughly washed, purged with sea-salt and vinegar for two hours, then after another copious rinsing, they have to be blanched for five or six minutes in boiling water. If they have been starved, do not cut off the black end. Put the drained snails in a pan and cover with the Chablis and stock. Add the *bouquet garni*, shallots and garlic, then season and pour in the brandy. Leave to simmer gently for three hours, then let the snails cool in their liquid. During this time prepare the snail butter, blending the garlic, shallots and parsley, all finely chopped together, with the seasoned butter. Pre-heat the oven to gas Mark 6-7 (210-230 °C. Fill the snails with the butter and arrange them on an oven-tray. Cover with the breadcrumbs and moisten with a little Chablis. Let the snails heat through, then turn the oven up very high. The snails should be served as soon as the butter starts to bubble."

Another speciality of the region is the chitterling sausage called *andouillette*. The best ones are sold by Michel Soulié in his shop at 3 bis, place du Général-de-Gaulle in Chablis (tel: 86 42 12 82). This great artist is heir to 120 years of expertise. Every one of his sausages is a joy. They are cut and tied by hand in the traditional manner. In 1978, Michel Soulié received the highest award: the "5 As" diploma of the Amicable Association of the Amateurs of Authentic Andouillettes, founded by Francis Amunatégui. Nothing could be simpler to cook than *andouillette*. You grill it as it is over a fire of chardonnay vine-prunings, sprinkling it with a little vinegar containing a few chopped shallots. It may also be prepared with Chablis wine: prick the sausage and brown it in butter in a frying-pan; leave it to cook for twenty minutes. Remove the sausage, add mustard, shallots, Chablis and a little salt and pepper to the pan, and stir well with a wooden spoon. Return the sausage to the pan and leave to cook for another ten minutes.

In general, Chablis is the crowning glory of any white wine sauce. But it would be a travesty to use it exclusively for culinary purposes. We have seen that Chablis wines go perfectly with fish, shellfish and crustacea. But, like all white wines, it is more or less killed by smoked salmon, whose oiliness is better neutralized on the palate by aquavit or vodka.

All white meats cooked in a sauce go well with Chablis, which stands up perfectly well to spicy dishes (even better than a champagne or a *rosé*) . With curried lamb, for example, however hot, a Chablis of not too old a vintage will be wonderful, whereas the best red wine would be killed. It is a well-nigh impossible challenge to find a wine to drink with asparagus, spinach, sorrel or broccoli. But the personality of the great Chablis wines renders them impervious to attack by such vegetables. They may be drunk perfectly well even with a green salad, especially if served with goat cheese, which should preferably be slightly warmed.

If you are looking for the very heart of local gastronomy, go to the Hôtel de l'Etoile in the centre of Chablis village. This restaurant was founded in 1851

by Bergerand, sauce-chef at the Tuileries under Louis-Philippe. Its fame has spread all over the world through its celebrated clientele. Alphonse XIII, the Aga Khan, Rockefeller, Sacha Guitry, Tristan Bernard and Mistinguett (to name but a few) often made their way there to drink *père* Bergerand's

▲ *The Porte Noël in Chablis is typical of the architecture of lower Burgundy.*

A painting by Madame Robert Fèvre, a charming and alert octogenarian, of "her" Chablis. ▶

Chablis wines with piping hot ham *à la maison*, fillet of sole, *andouillette* or
pike *quenelles* with Chablis. Doubtless inspired by so much excellence, Jean
Cocteau wrote *La Voix humaine* here in a single night. That was in 1930.
Today, Monsieur and Madame Roy, Charles Bergerand's nephew and niece,
maintain the restaurant's tradition of hospitality, keeping one of the best

tables in the Chablis region. In addition, Chablis has recently gained another first class hotel and restaurant – The Hostellerie des Clos – which has become very popular. Lastly, though in a completely different style – simpler but very warm and friendly – the Vieux Moulin restaurant should also be mentioned. Regional specialities also include *gougères* and "Duché" biscuits. The first are large choux puffs flavoured with cheese, which are ideal for "clearing the palate" at wine-tastings. Duché biscuits are to Chablis what humbugs are to Cambrai. Jacques Raveneau (16 rue Auxerroise, tel: 86 42 12 16) jealously guards the recipe, a family secret since 1830. The Duché biscuit has the distinction of keeping for a long time and yet still remaining crisp after being dipped in a glass of Chablis.

Gastronomy and folklore are faithful companions, twin products of a culture which sends its roots deep into the soil. Chablis has its troubadour in the person of one of its notaries, Maître René Sotty. It was thanks to him that the Brotherhood of the Piliers Chablisiens came into existence. He also deserves credit for the "moveable" festival of Saint-Vincent, the wine festival and the Regain choral and folk-dance group. He explains: "We wanted to create a special ceremonial preserving a typically Chablisian character. The essential thing was that everything should contribute to making the Chablis vignerons understand and acknowledge that they made up a firmly and closely knit entity." Maître Sotty began his festive activities with the foundation of the Regain group. That was in 1941, when twenty or so young people from Chablis joined him to give singing concerts in aid of prisoners of war. When peace returned, the choral group devoted itself to making the songs of the area better known, accompanied by musicians from Burgundy: Joseph Samson, Paul Berthier and Robert Jardillier, among others. Some ten years later, the Regain group took part in the first wine festival. They were an instant success. They then added dance to song and doubled their numbers with the addition of a team of dancers. The customs and costumes were re-created as in the time of Rétif de La Bretonne. There is no doubt about it: the Chablis Regain, which has travelled all over Europe, has been been the wine's best publicity agent for over twenty-five years . It was an inspiration on the part of Maître Sotty, who has an inventor's turn of mind. It was he who created "leasing by the bottle"; I shall leave it to him to explain how it works:

"A chap owns some land with the right to the Chablis appellation which he rents out, all with the approval of the *préfecture*, over nine years for a hundredweight or so of corn per hectare. Another bloke, young and not too flush, would like to start up a vineyard or to expand what he has, providing he can find something to buy, and that will of course involve him in debt. Finally, the first says to the second: 'A vine has a life of about forty-five years. So, you will plant my parcel of land at your expense, you will look after it and have what it yields for forty-five years, but I will remain the proprietor. At the end of the contract, you will hand me back the land, but meanwhile, every year you

Thanks to Maître René Sotty's learning, imagination and inititiative, traditional Chablis folklore is a living reality. ▶

Everyone lends a hand during the wine festival. Houses are decorated and costumes prepared with a meticulous eye to detail. The festive spirit is infectious, generating good humour all round, and bringing together people of all ages in a spirit of conviviality.

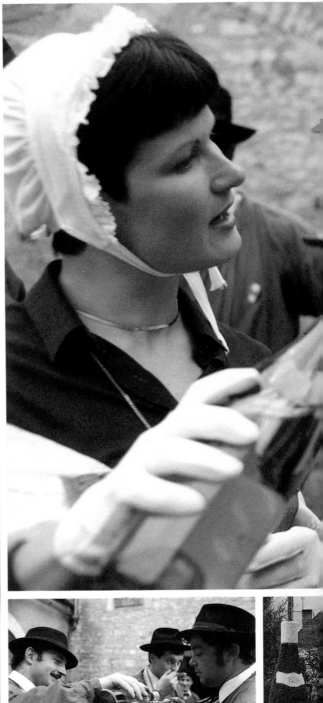

are to give me two or three bottles of the wine produced per *are* [120 square yards].' This system is to the advantage both of the lessor, who in this way can drink wine from his own property without paying for it, and the lessee, who can own vines without falling into the clutches of the Crédit Agricole.

"The idea took on rather rapidly and – *vox populi!* – was at once called 'leasing by the bottle'. But the two bottles per *are* soon became seven, eight, or even ten under fresh contracts. And the proprietor, feeling incapable, even with the assistance of his friends, of absorbing two or three thousand bottles every year, reserved himself the right to be paid their equivalent in monetary terms, at the prices charged by the lessee to his clients. After a few years, the agricultural service for the Department asked me to explain my invention to a young trainee of the Ecole Nationale d'Administration who had been given the job of looking into this innovation, unique in France. Confidently, and with a certain self-satisfaction, I explained the idea to her. I readily agreed that not everything could have been foreseen at the outset (for example, the introduction of VAT which was added to the price of the bottles) but that, because the affair had been conceived in a logical spirit, this same logical spirit would easily be able to resolve any ensuing problems. But the girl who, at twenty years of age, could not have been expected to have had much experience in viticultural matters (and of course remained blinkered by the rigid doctrines learned at university) wrote a pretty stiff report about it, coming to the conclusion that it would be better to ditch the whole system. The *préfet* rolls his eyes to heaven; for the rent received is obviously far greater than the traditional sums measured in corn. No one has taken the trouble to find out whether the procedure suits both parties who, as a general rule, are at each other's throats, but who in this case are mutually satisfied. The jurists seize the report. The Law Council deliberates but, more concerned with the splitting of hairs, will not admit that one of its members be allowed to be an innovator. No one asks the opinion of the parties concerned nor, obviously, my own."

Maître Sotty stops for a moment, with a far-away look. He smiles, thinking perhaps of the Regain group or the Piliers Chablisiens. Perhaps he is fortunate not to have been brought before the courts for founding a group of activists! He puts his glass of Mont de Milieu to his lips. A sip quickly brings him back to reality and he points heavenwards: "All I know is that thanks to my system, a number of young folk were able to plant four hundred or four hundred and fifty hectares of vines without incurring debt, and so also helped to re-create the market for Chablis wines. So much the worse for the jurists!"

To shed further light on the matter, I call as witness the late Pierre-Marie Doutrelant (*Les Bons Vins et les autres*, Editions du Seuil, 1976): "Chablis is not lacking in land for vines. Out of 5,500 hectares included in the appellation, scarcely 1,000 are planted. But the other 4,500 produce cereals, a crop which is said to give the most constant yield. The producers of corn jib at selling land to growers, or if they do so, it is at a very high price. One hectare of

vine land, which before 1970 was worth ten thousand francs, is today worth anything up to fifty thousand. The *Premiers Crus* can reach eighty thousand and the *Grands Crus*, one hundred thousand."

Over the last ten years things have changed again, for wine producers have found new prosperity, and for the moment, cereals give place to vines. Vines

▲ *Messieurs Goublot and Sotty are the true revivers of Chablis' community life. They have successfully united the traditions of the past with contemporary lifestyles.*

				Worth per bottle in 1989
40-50 F	65 F	70-90 F	110-115 F	
Petit Chablis	Chablis	Chablis 1ers Cru	Grands Crus	

are not yet being grubbed up to make way for wheat: on the contrary, and the prices suggested by P.-M. Doutrelant could do with being brought up to date, for they have rocketed. For evidence of this, you need look no further than at the soaring price of Chablis over thirty-five years.

The market in bottled wines represents about 30 per cent of the total production. For the rest, the unit of sale is the sacrosanct "feuillette" of 132 litres – a unit firmly rooted in commercial habits.

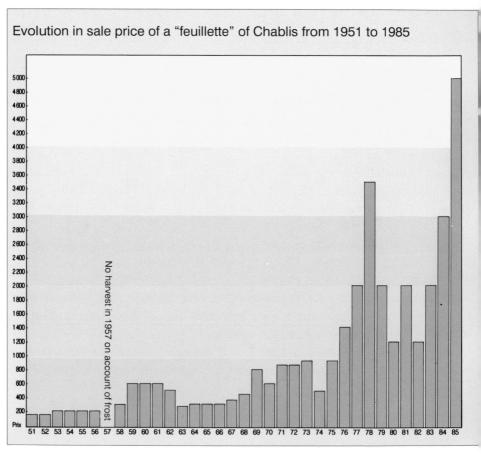

Evolution in sale price of a "feuillette" of Chablis from 1951 to 1985

Up to 1981, prices were fixed in a rather anarchic fashion according to supply and demand. Since 1982 the opening prices of each vintage have been determined by an agreement between the growers and the merchants. This attempt at regulating prices appears to work in favour of the producers. The 1985 vintage reached a historic peak, which remains relatively modest if we compare it with the prices of the Meursaults: 15,000 francs for the Meursault appellation and 18,000 francs for the *Premier Cru* Meursault. In Chablis, the *Premiers Crus* command a premium of about 50 per cent over the Chablis AOC, and the *Grands Crus*, 100 per cent.

Export markets account for at least 80 per cent of production. The United States absorbs the largest part. It is also the country in which the name of Chablis is most abused. No one can claim that the notion of what is commonly called "generic Chablis", that is a Chablis-style wine divorced from any conception of origin, helps Chablis' reputation. I share this view, while at the same time regretting that the people of Chablis, as well as the

---

▲ *An appalling example of American "Chablis". The can on the right is accompanied by four cream crackers and a portion of pasteurized cheese: a nice individual portion for your "wine and cheese party".* (Très bon!)

Impression on the seal of a Chablis bottle for export, certifying the source of its despatch. ▶

growers and merchants, have for a long time allowed such usages to take root. But we should be aware that the American consumer, while recognizing the style, differentiates sharply between "domestic Chablis" (especially those produced in California), "exotic Chablis" (coming from Spain or Australia) and French Chablis. The price of the genuine article alone distinguishes it from the others, so helping to dispel any ambiguity. Rosemary George, in the book I have already cited, uses a Daumier drawing showing two old codgers sitting in front of a bottle on a table, casting them in the roles of two old Californian growers chatting in a Napa Valley bar. In a confidential whisper, one of them says: "Do you know what I've just heard? Get this: they make Chablis in France as well!"

Catalogue

The number and complexity of the estates, and wine-producers of the Chablis region are such that they can be described only briefly here.

In this catalogue, all the growers of *Grand* and *Premier Cru* Chablis are mentioned. For the latter, our source is the National Interprofessional Wine Bureau (ONIVINS) in Dijon, whose director, Raymond Bernard, has been kind enough to draw up an exhaustive list of producers especially for this book. We have not indicated the total area under production for each one, for these figures vary from year to year depending on new plantings and renting out, or "métayage", which frequently change the size of the undertaking. The producers of Chablis and Petit-Chablis AOC have been listed according to the harvest return figures registered in each commune. It should be noted that the person making a return generally has his production registered in only one town hall even though it may come from different communes. At the end of the book, the general index enables the reader to find all the *climats* in which any one viticulturalist operates.

For the *Grands Crus* and *Premiers Crus*, the number of coloured glasses indicates the potential quality of the *climat* concerned. This estimate has been made according to the reputation of the *cru*, its natural agrological qualities and the personal opinion of the author. It can be subject to fluctuation, according to the particular success of any *climat* from year to year and according to the individual success of any one viticulturalist rather than another.

In Chablis, the spelling of place names can vary considerably in different reference sources (old or new land registers, local practice, phonetic transcription of pronunciation, spelling simplifications or, on the other hand, an attempt at creating an "olde worlde" effect). For example, the *Grand Cru* "Bougros" can be written Bougrot, Bougrots, Bouguerots, and even preceded by the definitive article. The *Premier Cru* "Trœsmes" , equally, may become Troëme, Troêmes, Trouesmes, etc. We have adopted the official spelling of these *climats* as approved by the INAO

Grands Crus

Some one hundred hectares contain the most distinguished of the Chablis names. They represent the *ne plus ultra* of quality and command a price 30% to 50% higher than the *Premiers Crus*. Production being limited by the modest extent of the appellation, *Grand Cru* wines are highly sought after all over the world. It should be noted that although their prices might seem high, they maintain a reasonable level compared to the great white lords of the Côte d'Or. In good years, the *Grands Crus* reach the very peak of quality. For the wine lover, a few bottles (which can keep quite happily) are an absolute must. As the accompaniment to a special meal, a *Grand Cru* will leave no guest unimpressed. The original character and the very distinctive personality of the seven Chablis princes unquestionably warrants them a place in the "Who's Who" of the best white wines in the world.

The *Grand Cru* slopes stretch out in a crescent along the right bank of the Serein opposite the village of Chablis. With a favourable south-south-west exposure, they benefit from the maximum amount of sunshine. In 1919, when viticulturalists and merchants set up a commission entrusted by the *Préfet* of the Yonne with the task of proposing an administrative delimitation for the Chablis *crus*, the idea of *Grand Cru* was officially realized. In fact it was already in existence, and this "promotion" simply gave recognition to a quality and distinction which had been unofficially acknowledged for centuries. In 1935, three years before the great laws of *Appellation d'origine*, Albert Pic drew up a list of the Chablis *climats*. Those which he designated "Top of the *Premiers Crus* " were Blanchot, Les Clos, Valmur, Grenouilles and Vaudésir. In 1938, Bougros and Preuses were also admitted to this elite club, which has not been modified since.

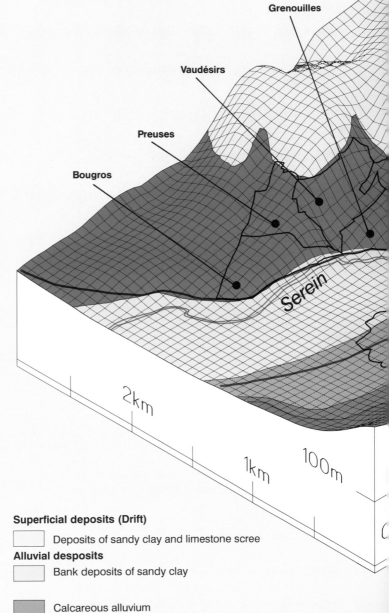

Chablis Grands Crus

Grenouilles

Vaudésirs

Preuses

Bougros

Serein

2km

1km

100m

Superficial deposits (Drift)

Deposits of sandy clay and limestone scree

Alluvial desposits

Bank deposits of sandy clay

Calcareous alluvium

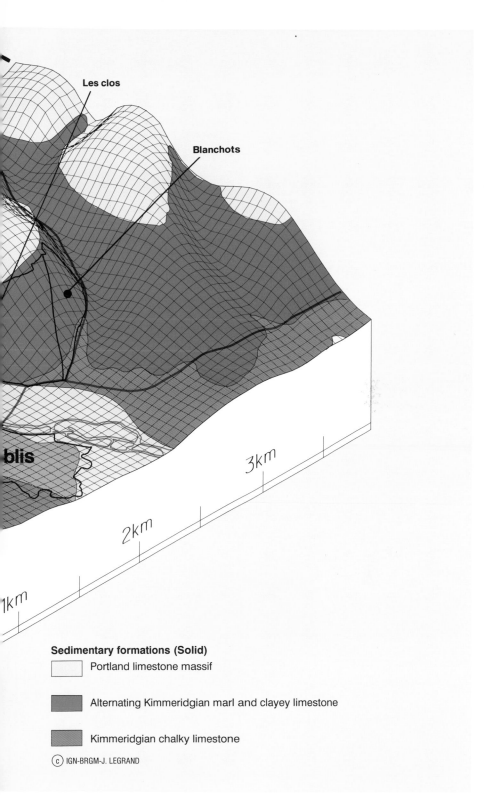

Sedimentary formations (Solid)

Portland limestone massif

Alternating Kimmeridgian marl and clayey limestone

Kimmeridgian chalky limestone

ⓒ IGN-BRGM-J. LEGRAND

Blanchot

♈♈♈♈♈

Spelt with or without an "s" at the end, Blanchot is the south-western rampart of the *Grand Cru* slopes. It makes up a total of 13.1 hectares. Blanchot wines are among the most delicate and perfumed. They can, and often do, have an exquisite lightness and a subtle bouquet. The old vines of the Domaines Laroche produce wonders.

Growers

Bègue, Maurice
6 rue A. Hovelacque, 89800 Chablis

Billaud, Jean & André
1 quai de Reugny, 89800 Chablis

Bouchard, Pascal
17 bd Lamarque, 89800 Chablis

Collet, Claude
10 rue A. Hovelacque, 89800 Chablis

Fenice, Paule
17 rue Paul Bert, 94160 Saint-Mandé

Fèvre, René
89800 Chablis

Laroche (SCEA)
67 Grande Rue, 89800 Maligny

Long Depaquit, Albert (Domaine)
45 rue Auxerroise, 89800 Chablis
The jewel of this reputable old firm is La Moutonne in Vaudésir. But it also has estates in Blanchot, Vaudésir, Les Clos and Preuses. Today, under Albert Bichot from Beaune and the enlightened management of Gérard Vullien, the Domaine Long Depaquit is a model of tradition and quality. All the firm's Grands Crus are bottled in Chablis; some bear the original label, others that of Bichot.

Moreau, Jean (Domaines)
Rue Auxerroise, 89800 Chablis

Raveneau, François
9 rue de Chichée, 89800 Chablis

Robin, Guy
13 rue Berthelot, 89800 Chablis

Servin, Bernard
3 avenue Jean Jaurès, 89800 Chablis

Servin (SCE)
20 av. d'Oberwesel, 89800 Chablis

Vocoret, R. (& Fils)
16 rue Emile Zola, 89800 Chablis
This has been a family business for more than a hundred years. The Vocorets are to be found all over Chablis wherever the best wines are produced. Among Grands Crus they are to be found in Blanchot, where they own about two hectares, and also in Les Clos and Valmur. In vinification they stick to the old methods. The wines are excellent, classic and unquestionably reliable.

Bougros

♈♈♈♈♈

The 15.9 hectares of Bougros in the north-western tip of the region along the road to Maligny. This *climat*, which is particularly susceptible to frost, is distinguished by the robust character of its wines, which can sometimes border on hardness.

Growers

Auffray (Ancien Domaine)
14 rue Jules Rathier, 89800 Chablis

Dupas, Henri
89800 Fontenay-près-Chablis

Filippi, Jeanne-Paule (SC)
14 rue Jules Rathier, 89800 Chablis

Gautheron, Jean-Michel
89800 Fontenay-près-Chablis

Drouhin, Joseph
1 rue d'Enfer, 21200 Beaune

Lafay, Thierry
5 rue du Panonceau, 89800 Chablis

Laroche (SCEA)
67 Grande Rue, 89800 Maligny

On William Fèvre's estate, everything breathes tradition.

Maladière (Domaine de la)
14 rue Jules Rathier, 89800 Chablis
On the Grand Cru *slopes, the principal interest of the president William Fèvre is in Bougros, where there are more than 6 hectares of vines, including those of Jeanne-Paule Filippi and the Ancien Domaine Auffray, which are all run together. In fact William Fèvre produces wines from all the* Grands Crus, *with the exception of Blanchot. The Fèvre vineyards cover about 16 hectares in all. The present owner is of noble ancestry, for his grandfather was a vigneron in the time of Restif de La Bretonne. He is proud of his origins, in Fontenay-près-Chablis. Today, this suburban "outsider" has been accepted as a fully-fledged Chablisien and William Fèvre is the true king of the* Grands Crus, *being at the same time the redoubtable champion of ageing in new wood. He claims, with a conviction so intense as to be almost evangelical, that the aromas of great Chablis cannot develop without the help of wood. The wines of William Fèvre are both austere and charming, rather in the drily humorous style of their maker? There is something about him which makes me think of Buster Keaton. In short, this is great artistry.*

Mignard, Christian
40 rue Auxerroise, 89800 Chablis

Mothe, Gilbert
89800 Fontenay-près-Chablis

Mothe, Guy
89800 Fontenay-près-Chablis

Mothe, Jean-Louis
89800 Fontenay-près-Chablis

Robin, Michel
2 rue du Puits, 89800 Chablis

Roy, Raymond & Claude
89800 Fontenay-près-Chablis

Servin (SCE)
20 av. d'Oberwesel, 89800 Chablis
The grandfather was a cooper with Simonnet, but he had his own small vineyard which within three generations has grown to over 15 hectares, of which approximately 3-5 are in Grand Cru *vineyards. Jean Servin has a practical and rather modern outlook: he was one of the first here to hire a mechanical harvester. The wines are not lacking in character.*

Vauroux (Domaine de)
89800 Chablis

Grenouilles

The wines of Grenouilles are more or less a synthesis of all the qualities of the *Grands Crus* . It is often difficult to distinguish them, but are notable for their generous, even overpowering bouquet. The terrain is in the middle of the *Grand Cru* slopes and covers just under 10 hectares. The estate of Château Grenouille, which used to belong to the Testut brothers, was divided a few years ago between several proprietors.

Growers

Château Grenouille (Domaine du)
89800 Chablis
Throughout the Grand Cru *slopes there is only one building to be seen a tumbledown sort of farm which some anonymous humorist one day dubbed Château Grenouille (Frog Castle). Between 1966 and 1979, after successive acquisitions, the estate came into the hands of the Testut family, well known in France as manufacturers of reliable weighing machines and scales. Philippe Testut, who waged his first campaign in the Chablis region with the firm of Long Depaquit, administered the estate for these thirteen years. But family problems arose and, after carefully weighing the pros and cons, the Testuts decided to sell. This created quite a stir and a great number of potential buyers. Finally a private limited company, composed of many local people, was set up, in order to buy the land, with the financial assistance of the Crédit Agricole. The* cave coopérative, La Chablisienne, *bought the buildings. So the estate of 7.2 hectares is now in the hands of a private company whose mem-*

bers include André Lecestre, Manuel de Oliveira, Ulysse Porcheron, Jean-Pierre Rousseau and Rémy Simonot. The marketing of this excellent Grand Cru *is carried out exclusively by La Chablisienne.*

Droin, Jean-Paul
14 bis rue Jean Jaurès, 89800 Chablis
Jean-Paul Droin is the ninth generation of viticulturalists in direct line. Helped by his wife Catherine, he manages 16 hectares of splendid vines in Grands Crus *(Valmur, Vaudésir, Grenouilles, Les Clos) and in* Premiers Crus *(Montée de Tonnerre, Vaillons, Montmain, Vosgros, Fourchaume, Côte de Léchet, Vaucoupin).*

He has just built a stone cellar to enable him to age his wines in wood as a matter of course. Jean-Paul Droin's wines are always reliable.

Gautherin, Raoul
6 bd Lamarque, 89800 Chablis

Maladière (Domaine de la)
14 rue Jules Rathier, 89800 Chablis

Michel, Louis (& Fils)
11 bd des Ferrières, 89800 Chablis
After the "Château", the Michels are the most significant modern in Grenouilles. They own approximately 0.55 hectares and have vines in Vaudésir and Les Clos, run with the lively interest and concern of a family with an eye to perfection. The wines produced by Louis and Jean-Loup Michel are exemplary and superb.

Testut Frères (SCEA)
Ch. de Grenouille, 89800 Chablis

Les Clos

♀ ♀ ♀ ♀ ♀

It was most probably at Les Clos that viticulture in Chablis its first began. With 27 hectares, it is the largest of the *Grands Crus* . Its wine is also the most typical, thanks to its complex, deep and suave character. Le Clos des Hospices, which belongs to the firm of J. Moreau & Fils, is in a way to Les Clos what La Moutonne is to Vaudésir, that is to say, a quite distinctive microclimate.

Growers

Auffray (Ancien Domaine)
14 rue Jules Rathier, 89800 Chablis

Billaud, Jean & André
1 quai de Reugny, 89800 Chablis

Bouchard, Pascal
17 bd Lamarque, 89800 Chablis

Dauvissat, René
8 rue Emile Zola, 89800 Chablis

De Oliveira & Lecestre
89800 Fontenay-près-Chablis

Droin Jean-Paul
14 bis rue Jean Jaurès, 89800 Chablis

Drouhin, Joseph (SC)
1 rue d'Enfer, 21200 Beaune

Duplessis Père & Fils
5 quai de Reugny, 89800 Chablis

Feuillebois, René
13 rue de Reugny, 89800 Chablis

Fèvre, Maurice
17 av. A. Briand, 89800 Chablis

Filippi, Jeanne-Paule (SC)
14 rue Jules Rathier, 89800 Chablis

Gautherin, Raoul
6 bd Lamarque, 89800 Chablis

Jacquin, Jean
30 rue de Chichée, 89800 Chablis

Laroche (SCEA)
67 Grande Rue, 89800 Maligny

Lavens, Michel
45 HLM Les Picards, 89800 Chablis

Long Depaquit, Albert (Domaine)
45 rue Auxerroise, 89800 Chablis

Maladière (Domaine de la)
14 rue Jules Rathier, 89800 Chablis

Michel, Louis (& Fils)
11 bd des Ferrières, 89800 Chablis

Michel, Maurice
9 rue Emile Zola, 89800 Chablis

Moreau, Jean (Domaines)
Rue Auxerroise, 89800 Chablis
A longer description of the firm of Moreau is given in the section dealing

Pruning the vines at the foot of Les Clos.

with négociants, but it also deserves its place in the Grands Crus and, more particularly, in Les Clos where it reigns over 7 hectares. Within this substantial vineyard is a stronghold of quality called "Le Clos des Hospices", which can be compared to La Moutonne in Vaudésir. The 2 hectares of this micro-estate come from the estate owned by the Hôpital de Chablis until the Revolution. The use of the name "Clos des Hospices" goes back way beyond the first laws regarding AOCs. Today, though its legal structure might appear ambiguous to some, Le Clos des Hospices can claim a history stretching over a thousand years. Can many do better? This is an example of how the reputation of a cru can overshadow that of its climat. A third of the vines of Le Clos des Hospices are 35 years old and the other two thirds, 20 years old. Their yields are modest: between 20 and 40 hectolitres per hectare, depending on the year. In my opinion the price of the wine is justified by a well-nigh constant perfection. Let those who complain go elsewhere if they think they can find better!

Pinson, Louis
2 rue Vieilles Boucheries, Chablis

Pinson (SCEA du Domaine)
5 quai Voltaire, 89800 Chablis

Raveneau, François
9 rue de Chichée, 89800 Chablis
A well-known and popular figure in the region, Raveneau has vines in Les Clos, Valmur and Blanchot. More often than not, his wines are the quintessence of great Chablis and they need to be kept rather a long time in the bottle. Wines with the Raveneau label are highly recommended to the connoisseur.

Servin (SCE)
20 av. d'Oberwesel, 89800 Chablis

Tremblay, André
89800 La Chapelle-Vaupelteigne

Vocoret, R. (& Fils)
16 Rue Emile Zola, 89800 Chablis

Preuses ♟♟♟♟♟

Bougros and Preuses were received into the "Grands" in 1938. The 11.8 hectares of the Preuses vineyards are an extension of Bougros towards the top of the slopes. Generally, the wine it produces is considered the easiest of the *Grands Crus*, doubtless because of its "roundness" which tends to give an impression of fullness. This characteristic makes it an agreeable wine even in off-years.

Growers

Billaud, Jean & André
1 quai de Reugny, 89800 Chablis

Dauvissat, Jean
89800 Chablis

Dauvissat, René
8 rue Emile Zola, 89800 Chablis

Drouhin, Joseph (SC)
1 rue d'Enfer, 21200 Beaune

Dupas, Henri
89800 Fontenay-près-Chablis
After William Fèvre (Domaine de la Maladière), Henri Dupas is the largest vineyard owner in Preuses. He is an old and faithful member of the cave coopérative, La Chablisienne, whose standards of quality he easily meets: his substantial contributions are the result of meticulous care.

Fèvre Frères (GAEC)
89800 Fontenay-près-Chablis

Filippi, Jeanne-Paule (SC)
14 rue Jules Rathier, 89800 Chablis

La Moutonne (GFA)
89800 Chablis

Long Depaquit, Albert (GFA)
45 rue Auxerroise, 89800 Chablis

Maladière (Domaine de la)
14 rue Jules Rathier, 89800 Chablis

Roy, Raymond & Claude
89800 Fontenay-près-Chablis
The son and grandson of vignerons from Fontenay, Raymond Roy is a grower in the Preuses and Bougros Grands Crus, and at Couverte, Les Côtes and Vaulorent Premiers Crus. He maintains his vines carefully with the help of his wife Raymonde and son Claude, whose wife is called Annie. They have about 10 hectares of good

land, but they have not had the time to develop their direct sales, which at present are limited to a few friends and acquaintances. The bulk of their production is faithfully bought up every year by the firm of Moreau in Chablis. Up to 1973, harvesting was done by a cheerful team of pickers from Denmark. The mechanical harvester has ousted them, apart from two or three survivors who come along to "give a hand". It is sometimes said in Chablis that Raymond Roy is a difficult man. Raymond, who ought to know, would reply that he prefers people to tread his grapes rather than tread on his toes. That is understandable.

Servin, Bernard
3 av. Jean Jaurès, 89800 Chablis

Servin (SCE)
20 av. d'Oberwesel, 89800 Chablis

Valmur ♟♟♟♟♟

This glorious *climat* of 12.9 hectares reigns supreme among its peers. It produces rather firmly structured wines which nevertheless do not lack suppleness. In good years, Valmur is ideally suitable for ageing. It enjoys a remarkable success in Anglo-Saxon countries.

Growers

Auffray (Ancien Domaine)
14 rue Jules Rathier, 89800 Chablis

Collet, Jean (& Fils)
1 rue du Panonceau, 89800 Chablis
Jean Collet, Grand Architrave of the Piliers Chablisiens, is a natural phenomenon whose stature commands respect. So do his wines. He is mainly a grower of Premiers Crus, but he is particularly attached to his three parcels in Valmur which make up nearly half a hectare.

Droin Jean-Paul
14 bis rue Jean Jaurès, 89800 Chablis

Maladière (Domaine de la)
14 rue Jules Rathier, 89800 Chablis

Moreau, Jean (Domaines)
Rue Auxerroise, 89800 Chablis

Moreau, Roger
5 rue des Fossés, 89800 Chablis

Raveneau, Jean-Marie
9 rue de Chichée, 89800 Chablis

Robin, Guy
13 rue Berthelot, 89800 Chablis
The Robins are an old Chablis family. Helped by his son Jean-Pierre, Guy Robin is one of the largest proprietors in Valmur and also has vines in Blanchot and Vaudésir. He is a fierce ad-

vocate of fermentation in the cask. All his Grands Crus are aged in wood, which gives them a fine, firm structure and a bouquet of complex aromas. His best vintages are masterpieces.

Rottiers, Clotilde (Domaine)
61 rue Auxerroise, 89800 Chablis

Tremblay, Louis
89800 La Chapelle-Vaupelteigne

Vocoret R. (& Fils)
16 rue Emile Zola, 89800 Chablis

Vaudésir   �♟ ♟ ♟ ♟ ♟

Pride of place here must undoubtedly go to the principality of La Moutonne, whose 2.6 hectares straddle Preuses and Vaudésir. This, as I have said elsewhere, is perhaps the Chablis region's most celebrated private label. Vaudésir as a whole covers 16.2 hectares, situated between the almost equally famous slopes of Preuses and Valmur. The wines it produces are sinewy, and distinguished by their freshness and finesse. Their fruit and authentic flavour of their *terroir* make them the favourite of many Chablis lovers (myself amongst them).

Growers

Besson, Alain
19 rue Emile Zola, 89800 Chablis

Besson, Félix-Pierre
28 rue de Reugny, 89800 Chablis
This thoroughbred grower "started in the vines" at the age of 14. Even before doing his National Service, he already owned a few small parcels. After patient acquisitions of land he now has vineyards not only in Vaudésir but also in the Premiers Crus Montmains, Vaillons *and* Mont de Milieu. *Strangely enough, his top-grade production, Vaudésir, is sold in bulk to the merchants, whereas his other wines are bought up partly by passing trade but mostly by the United States and Japan. The wines are vinified in enamelled steel and then bottled in the month of August. Félix Besson is helped by his son Alain, the two of them together making a solid team with a well-deserved reputation.*

Billaud, Jean & André
1 quai de Reugny, 89800 Chablis

Droin Jean-Paul,
14 bis rue Jean Jaurès, 89800 Chablis

Drouhin, Joseph (SC)
1 rue d'Enfer, 21200 Beaune

Fèvre, René
89800 Chablis

Filippi, Jeanne-Paule (SC)
14 rue Jules Rathier, 89800 Chablis

Gautherin, Raoul
6 bd Lamarque, 89800 Chablis
Approximately 12 hectares of Premiers Crus *supplement the 13,000 m2 of* Grand Cru *land owned by the Gautherin family, mainly in Vaudésir,* Les Clos *and* Grenouilles. *Today, Raoul Gautherin is helped by his son Alain who has studied oenology. These two generations combine tradition and progress hand in hand. Here, the big spender and the small buyer alike will find the same warm reception and a wine of good, consistent quality.*

La Moutonne (GFA)
89800 Chablis

The valley of Vaudésir shows clearly the effect of microclimates.

Lafay, Thierry
5 rue du Panonceau, 89800 Chablis

Long Depaquit, Albert (GFA)
45 rue Auxerroise, 89800 Chablis

Maladière (Domaine de la)
14 rue Jules Rathier, 89800 Chablis

Malandes (Domaine des)
Rue Auxerroise, 89800 Chablis

Michel, Louis (& Fils)
11 bd des Ferrières, 89800 Chablis

Moreau, Jean (Domaines)
Rue Auxerroise, 89800 Chablis

Reynier, Joseph
9 Furze Hill, Purley, Surrey

Robin, Guy
13 rue Berthelot, 89800 Chablis

Tremblay, André
89800 La Chapelle-Vaupelteigne

Premiers Crus

"The wines of the *Grands Crus*, the *Premiers Crus*, and those called simply Chablis have the same colour, the same limpidity and sometimes even the same body. What distinguishes them from each other is their finesse, their bouquet and the extent to which they are 'long in the mouth', that is to say, the length of time their savour remains in the mouth of the taster. They are also distinguishable by their more or less excellent propensity for ageing and by the resultant disparate tastes." This is how William Fèvre endeavours to marry the subjectivity of taste with the objectivity of the AC system.

As practice and legislation stand at the moment (the latter not yet having caught up with the former, the notion of *Premier Cru* is slightly less strictly defined than that of *Grand Cru*. Unlike a *Premier Cru*, a *Grand Cru* always mentions its *climat* of origin. The *Premiers Crus* which actually appear as names on the label are generally only those which are the most well known. However, intermarriage can often take place between a famous *Premier Cru* and its near neighbours. For example, Vaupulent and L'Homme Mort are frequently grouped together under the distinguished name of Fourchaume, and Côte de Bréchain, Pied d'Aloue and even Chapelot can all meet under the prestigious flag of Montée de Tonnerre. This might shock the purists. Although it is established practice here, it would not be a good idea for the habit to spread. On the other hand, it is clear that an owner of three small parcels in three different *climats* will want for reasons of both quality and good business, to make a single homogeneous wine. This combination of the three, doubtless better than each separate constituent element (the whole being greater than the sun of its parts), theoretically and even legally loses its idea of delimited origin. The grower who owns 0.40 hectares in Les Butteaux, one and a half hectares in Les Landes and Verjuts and one hectare in the Côte de Cuissy will do nothing for his reputation as a grower by offering his clients quantities rigorously in accord with the production of each of the three *climats*. So in such a case, in principle, he will call his blend quite simply *Premier Cru* without pinpointing it further geographically. It is in this spirit that the 1967 regulations (rather fluid, it is true) have been superseded by the provisions drawn up in 1978: "Only wines produced in those areas of land designated as *Premier Cru* may have their communal appellation further qualified either by the *climat* of origin, or by the expression "Premier Cru", or by both. The name of the *climat* of origin must be placed after the communal appellation and printed in letters whose dimensions, both in height and breadth should not exceed those of the appellation."

To gain as clear an idea as possible of the origin of the *Premiers Crus* marketed by any one producer, reference should be made to the following catalogue. The general index at the end of the book lists all the *climats* in which any one vine-grower is proprietor (or is in business, the two ideas having become confused). It is then up to the reader to draw the two together.

    The majority of the individual listings are based on the data collected by Rosemary George in her research on Chablis. The geographical atlas of the *Premiers Crus* which opens this section has been drawn up from the land registers and the boundaries kindly provided by the INAO in Dijon.

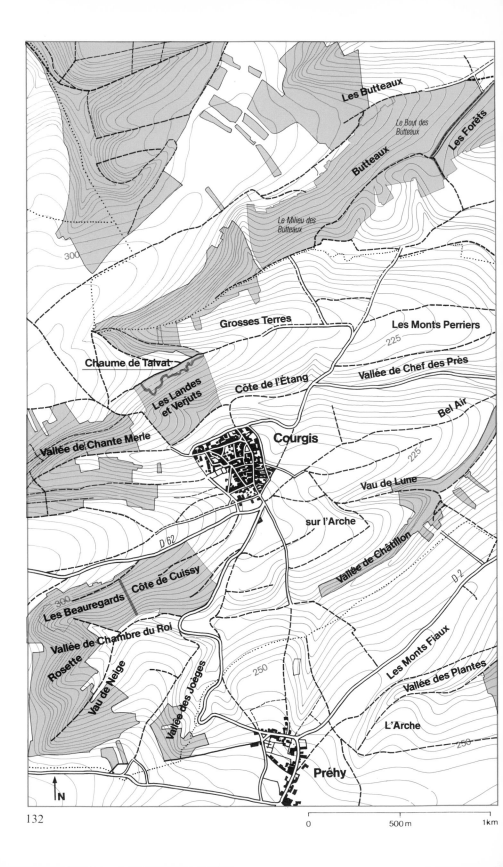

Les Butteaux

Le Bout des Butteaux

Les Forêts

Butteaux

Le Milieu des Butteaux

300

Grosses Terres

Les Monts Perriers

225

Chaume de Talvat

Vallée de Chef des Prés

Les Landes et Verjuts

Côte de l'Étang

Bel Air

Vallée de Chante Merle

Courgis

225

Vau de Lune

sur l'Arche

D 62

Vau de Lune

Vallée de Châtillon

D 2

Côte de Cuissy

Les Beauregards

300

Vallée de Chambre du Roi

Les Monts Fiaux

Rosette

Vallée des Plantes

Vau de Neige

250

L'Arche

Vallée des Joèges

250

Préhy

N

0   500 m   1km

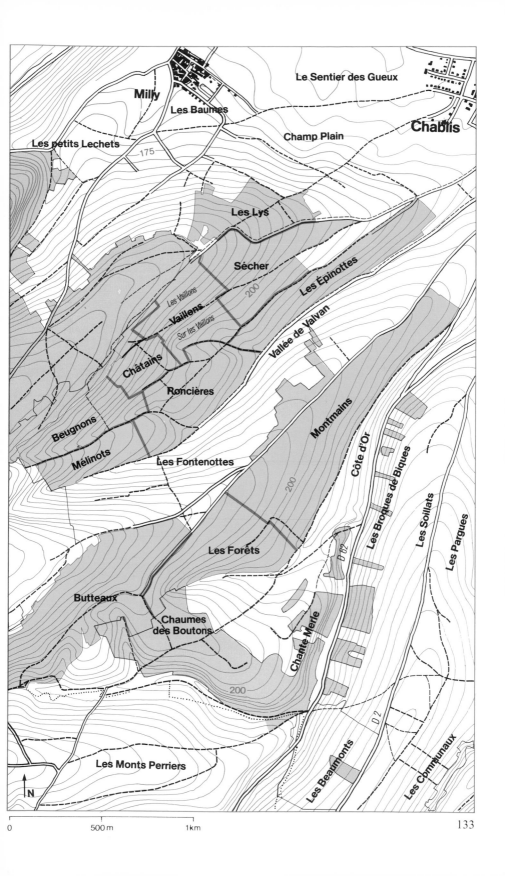

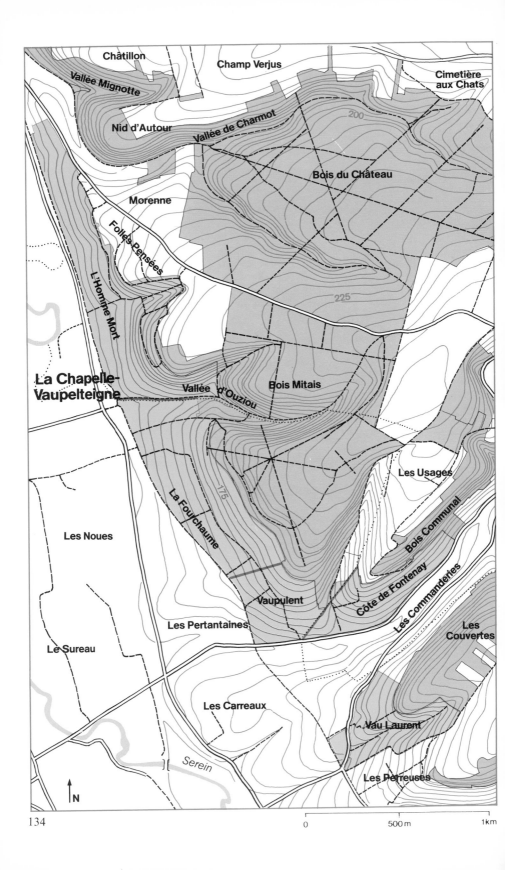

Châtillon

Champ Verjus

Cimetière
aux Chats

Vallée Mignotte

Nid d'Autour

Vallée de Charmot

200

Bois du Château

Morenne

Folles Pensées

225

L'Homme Mort

La Chapelle-
Vaupelteigne

Vallée d'Ouziou

Bois Mitais

175

Les Usages

La Fourchaume

Les Noues

Bois Communal

Côte de Fontenay

Les Commanderies

Vaupulent

Les Pertantaines

Les
Couvertes

Le Sureau

Les Carreaux

Vau Laurent

Serein

Les Perreuses

N

0   500 m   1 km

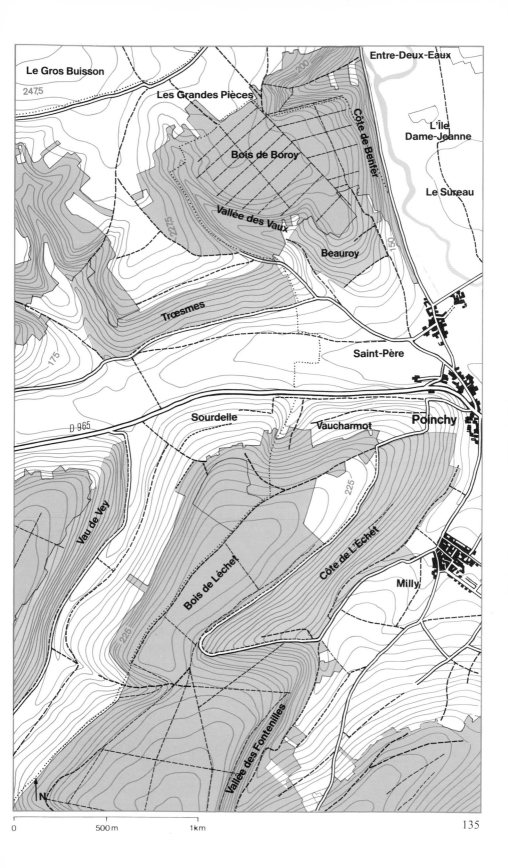

Le Gros Buisson

247,5

Entre-Deux-Eaux

Les Grandes Pièces

Côte de Benfer

L'Île
Dame-Jeanne

Bois de Boroy

Le Sureau

Vallée des Vaux

225,5

Beauroy

150

Trœsmes

175

Saint-Père

Sourdelle

D 965

Vaucharmot

Poinchy

225

Vau de Vey

Bois de Léchet

Côte de L'Échet

Milly

225

Vallée des Fontenilles

N

0   500 m   1km

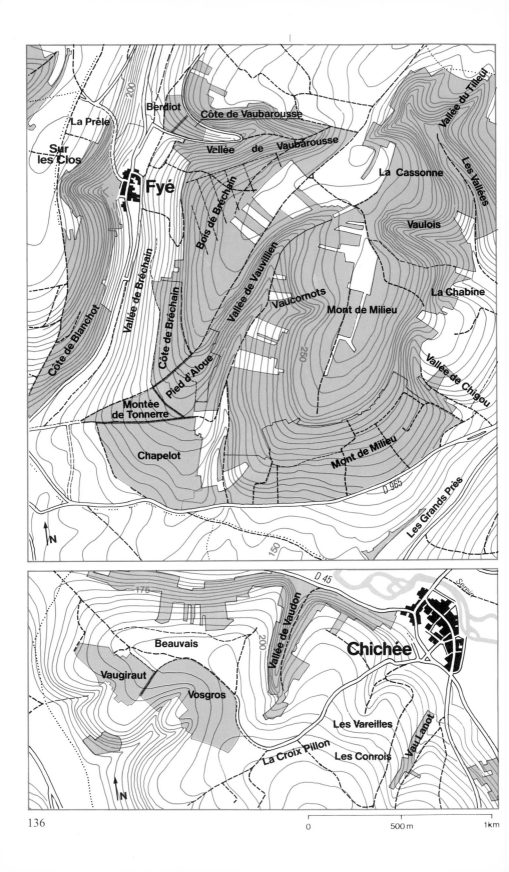

0   500 m   1km

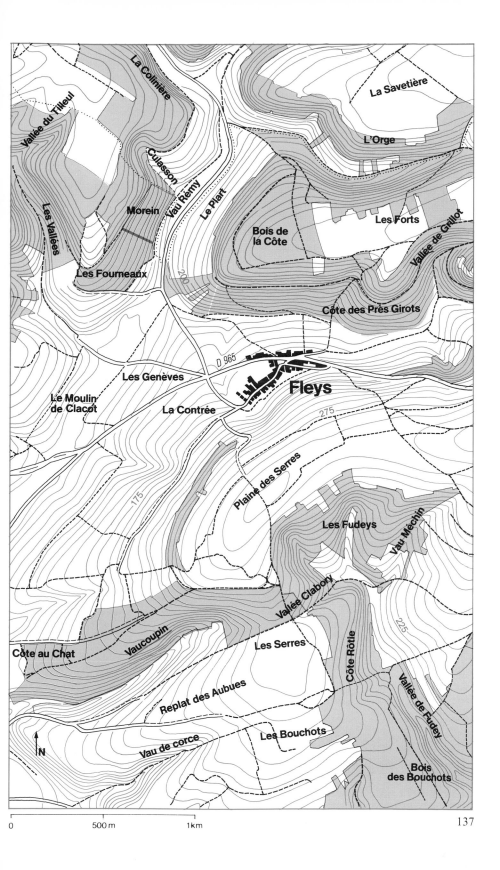

La Colinière
La Savetière
Vallée du Tilleul
L'Orge
Culasson
Vau Rémy
Le Plart
Morein
Les Forts
Vallée de Grillot
Bois de
la Côte
Les Vallées
Les Fourneaux
200
Côte des Prés Girots
D 965
Les Genèves
Fleys
Le Moulin
de Clacot
La Contrée
275
Plaine des Serres
175
Les Fudeys
Vau Méchin
Vallée Clabony
Côte au Chat
Vaucoupin
Les Serres
Côte Rôtie
Vallée de Fudey
225
Replat des Aubues
N
Vau de corce
Les Bouchots
Bois
des Bouchots

0   500 m   1km

137

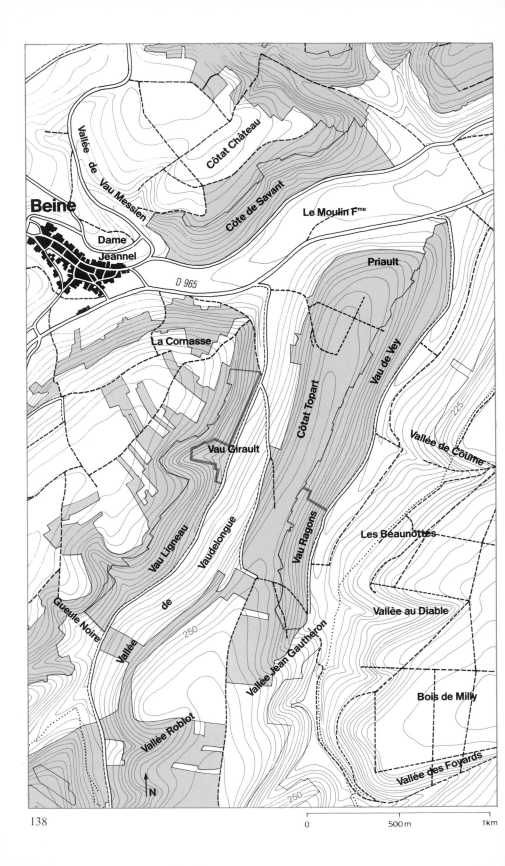

Beine

Vallée de Vau Messien

Côtat Château

Côte de Savant

Le Moulin Fᵐᵉ

Priault

Dame Jeannel

D 965

La Cornasse

Vau de Vey

Côtat Topart

Vallée de Coume

225

Vau Girault

Vau Ligneau

Vaudelongue

de

Vau Ragons

Les Béanottes

Gueule Noire

Vallée

250

Vallée Jean Gautheron

Vallée au Diable

Vallée Roblot

Bois de Milly

N

250

Vallée des Foyards

0   500 m   1 km

Beauroy

ΨΨΨΨΨ

Commune: Poinchy. **Named vineyards:** Sous Boroy, Vallée des Vaux, Benfer. **Area under production:** approximately 6 hectares. **Map:** page 135. This is a very old *Premier Cru* which used to be within the commune of Poinchy, but is today attached to Chablis. The wines are firm and vigorous, and age well. At the beginning of the century, the Beauroy appellation was highly esteemed. Today it is less well known. This is a pity.

Growers

Bouchard, Pascal
17 bd Lamarque, 89800 Chablis

Chatelain, Claude
89800 Poinchy

Dupas, Guy
89800 Chablis

Fèvre, Régis
89800 Fyé

Fouinat, Roland
89700 Tonnerre

Fromont-Moindrot
8 r. G. Dupas, 89800 Ligny-le-Châtel
The main part of the Fromont-Moin-drot estate is in Beauroy, where the family owns about three hectares, remarkably well placed in the best part of the climat *which corresponds to the vineyards known as "Sous Boroy".*

Hamelin, Marc (Domaine)
89800 Lignorelles

Jannet, Henri
89800 Poinchy

Maladière (Domaine de la)
14 rue Jules Rathier, 89800 Chablis

Morin, Jacques
89800 Poinchy

Simonot, Rémy
4 rue Troemes, 89800 Chablis

Harvesting in Beauroy. At the foot of the hill is the artificial lake.

Berdiot

ΨΨΨΨΨ

Commune: Fyé. **Named vineyard:** Berdiot. **Area under production:** approximately 1 hectare. **Map:** page 136. Berdiot lies within the former small vineyards of Fyé, now absorbed by the commune of Chablis. This *climat,* which faces mainly westwards, is a continuation of the Côte de Vaubarousse, above the valley of Bréchain. The name is practically unused, but the terrain is undoubtedly of good geological quality.

139

Beugnons ♀♀♀♀♀

Commune: Chablis. **Named vineyard:** Les Beugnons. **Area under production:** approximately 12 hectares. **Map:** page 133. At the south-western tip of the largest of the *Premiers Crus* ranges on the left bank, Beugnons borders on Mélinots, Châtains and Roncières. It is a *climat* which enjoys a long-established and high reputation and it tends to have a certain firmness, sometimes to the detriment of delicacy.

Growers	Bègue, Jean 11 rue Jules Rathier, 89800 Chablis	Long Depaquit, Albert (GFA) 45 rue Auxerroise, 89800 Chablis
Barat, Michel 89800 Milly *Of all Michel Barat's production, the most important is in the* Premier Cru *of Côte de Léchet, where he carefully cultivates over two hectares. But he also has well-placed land in Mont de Milieu, Vaillons, Beugnons, Les Fourneaux and Côte des Près Girots. So Michel Barat can offer a wide range of* climat *crus, whose quality is entirely to be recommended.*	**Besson, Félix** 28 rue de Reugny, 89800 Chablis	**Race, Denis** 16 rue de Chichée, 89800 Chablis
	Bourcey, Roland 89800 Milly	**Raoult, Eliane** Vezannes, 89700 Tonnerre
	Coulaudin, Henri 89800 Milly	**Robin, Jean-Pierre** 13 rue Berthelot, 89800 Chablis
	Dauvissat, René 8 rue Emile Zola, 89800 Chablis	**Villetard, Pierre** 13 rue de Léchet, 89800 Chablis
Bègue, Charles 12 rue de Chitry, 89800 Chablis	**Defaix, Daniel** 89800 Milly	
Bègue, Daniel 89700 Tonnerre	**Defaix, Etienne** 89800 Milly	
	Defaix, Jean 89800 Milly	

Butteaux ♀♀♀♀♀

Commune: Chablis. **Named vineyards:** Le Bout des Butteaux, Le Milieu des Butteaux, Les Ecueillis, Vaugerlains, Vaux Miolot. **Area under production:** approximately 40 hectares. **Map:** page 132. Butteaux is a large Chablis *climat* divided in two by part of Forêt on the left bank. Its name is rarely to be encountered commercially, as it is more often than not linked to Forêt. This is not as strange as it sounds, for it belongs to the same hillside and has the same geological, morphological and climatic conditions.

Growers	Auffray (Ancien Domaine) 14 rue Jules Rathier, 89800 Chablis	Bouc, Gabriel Route de Préhy, 89800 Chablis
Adine, Christian 89800 Courgis	**Barbier, Pierre** Rue Jeannette Rousseau, Chablis	**Chalmeau, Jacques** 89530 Saint-Bris-le-Vineux
Adine, Madeleine Rue Nicolas Droin, 89800 Chablis	**Besson, Alain** 19 rue Emile Zola, 89800 Chablis	**Chalmeau, Robert** 89530 Saint-Bris-le-Vineux
Adine, Maurice 89800 Courgis	**Besson, Felix** 28 rue de Reugny, 89800 Chablis	**Chapotin, Martine** 89800 Courgis

Charlet, Bernard
3 av. Paul-Eluard, 93000 Bobigny

Colbois, Daniel
89530 Saint-Bris-le-Vineux

Collet, Claude
10 rue A. Hovelacque, 89800 Chablis

Collet, Jean (& Fils)
1 rue du Panonceau, 89800 Chablis

Dupré, André
89800 Courgis

Feuillebois, Jean
89800 Chablis

Fèvre, Régis
89800 Fyé

Foulley, Philippe
Rue Jacques Ferrand, 89800 Courgis

Gautherin, Raoul
6 bd Lamarque, 89800 Chablis

George, Michel
Rue Jacques Ferrand, 89800 Chablis

Jacque, Odette
89800 Courgis

Landais, Roger
89800 Courgis

Laroche (SCEA)
67 Grande Rue, 89800 Maligny

Legland, Bernard
89800 Préhy
This young viticulturalist has devoted himself mainly to serving the French market; in ten years, he has made an enviable commercial success with the name "Domaine des Maronniers", covering wines which are very modern in style, mainly bearing the label Montmains. Most of his Premier Cru *vineyards are in Les Butteaux, Les Landes and Verjuts. His wines with the simple Chablis AOC appellation generally have a rich bouquet and quite a distinctive character.*

Lhéritier, Yves
14 rue Chaude, 89530 Saint-Bris

Maladière (Domaine de la)
14 rue Jules Rathier, 89800 Chablis

Michel, Louis (& Fils)
11 bd des Ferrières, 89800 Chablis

Moreau, René
5 rue des Fossés, 89800 Chablis

Picq, Georges
Gde Rue N. Droin, 89800 Courgis

Race, Alexandre
Grande Rue, 89800 Chablis

Race, Bernard
Rue Jacques Ferrand, 89800 Courgis

Race, Denis
16 rue de Chichée, 89800 Chablis

Race, Gilbert
Rue des Pressoirs, 89800 Courgis

Race, Rémy
89800 Courgis

Race, Suzanne
14 rue de Chichée, 89800 Chablis

Raveneau, Jean-Marie
9 rue de Chichée, 89800 Chablis

Rétif, Pierre
89800 Courgis

Robin, Guy
13 rue Berthelot, 89800 Chablis

Robin, Jean
89800 Chichée

Servin (SCE)
20 av. d'Oberwesel, 89800 Chablis

Sorin de France
11 bis rue de Paris, 89530 Saint-Bris

Tribaudaut, André
9 rue de la République, Chablis

Vocoret, Patrice
15 rue du Panonceau, 89800 Chablis

Vocoret, R. (& ses Fils)
16 rue Emile Zola, 89800 Chablis

Chapelot ♟ ♟ ♟ ♟ ♟

Commune: Fyé. **Named vineyard:** Les Chapelots. **Area under production:** approximately 20 hectares. **Map:** page 136. This *climat* has a remarkably favoured aspect, at the foot of the slopes on the right bank of the Serein. It therefore benefits from a position which is exactly comparable with that of the *Grands Crus*, of which it is one of the closest neighbours. It is a pity that it does not impose its own personality more than it does, being content to hide behind the name of Montée de Tonnerre.

Growers

Billaud, Jean & André
1 quai de Reugny, 89800 Chablis

Drouhin, Joseph
1 rue d'Enfer, 21200 Beaune

Durup, Jean
Dne de l'Eglantière, 89800 Chablis

Gouailhardou, Jean-Pierre
18 rue Auxerroise, 89800 Chablis

Jacquin, Jean
30 rue de Chichée, 89800 Chablis

Maladière (Domaine de la)
14 rue Jules Rathier, 89800 Chablis

Michel, Louis (& Fils)
11 bd des Ferrières, 89800 Chablis

Moreau, Roger
5 rue des Fossés, 89800 Chablis

Raveneau, Bernard
18 rue du Panonceau, 89800 Chablis

Raveneau, François
9 rue de Chichée, 89800 Chablis

Raveneau, Jean-Marie
9 rue de Chichée, 89800 Chablis

Robin, Guy
13 rue Berthelot, 89800 Chablis

Rogié, André
Chemin des Petits Dieux, Chablis

Soupé, Michelle
32 rue d'Oberwesel, 89800 Chablis

Vocoret, Patrice
15 rue du Panonceau, 89800 Chablis

Vocoret, R. (& Fils)
16 rue Emile Zola, 89800 Chablis

Châtains   ♈♈♈♈♈

Commune: Chablis. **Named vineyards:** Les Grands Chaumes, Les Châtains, Châtains. **Area under production:** approximately 15 hectares. **Map:** page 133. Across the Serein again, but without leaving the commune of Chablis, to these vineyards between Beugnons and Vaillons, where the microclimate is relatively cool and produces a splendidly austere wine, frequently assimilated into Vaillons.

Growers	Dauvissat, René 8 rue Emile Zola, 89800 Chablis	Maladière (Domaine de la) 14 rue Jules Rathier, 89800 Chablis
Abbaze, Mohamed 89800 Milly	Defaix, Jean 89800 Milly	Moreau, Jean (Domaines) Rue Auxerroise, 89800 Chablis
Bègue, Charles 12 rue de Chitry, 89800 Chablis	Duplessis Père & Fils 5 quai de Reugny, 89800 Chablis	Pinson (SCEA du Domaine) 5 quai Voltaire, 89800 Chablis
Bègue, Maurice 6 rue A. Hovelacque, 89800 Chablis	Feuillebois, Jean 13 rue de Reugny, 89800 Chablis	Robin, Michel 2 rue du Puits, 89800 Chablis
Billaud, Jean &André 1 quai de Reugny, 89800 Chablis	Feuillebois, René 6 rue de Montmain, 89800 Chablis	Vocoret, R. (& Fils) 16 rue Emile Zola, 89800 Chablis
Collet, Jean (& Fils) 1 rue du Panonceau, 89800 Chablis	Filippi, Jeanne-Paule (SC) 14 rue Jules Rathier, 89800 Chablis	
Coulandin, Fernand (Mme Veuve) 89800 Milly	Fourrey, Jean-Jack 89800 Milly	
Dauvissat, Jean (SCEA) 89800 La Chapelle-Vaupelteigne	La Fourchaume (GAEC de) 89800 La Chapelle-Vaupelteigne	
Dauvissat, Jean 89800 Chablis	Lavens, Jean-Mary Chemin du Moulin, 89800 Chablis	

Chaume de Talvat   ♈♈♈♈♈

To the north of the commune of Courgis, this *Premier Cru* has been completely assimilated into Les Landes and Verjuts. Its land is of variable viticultural quality.

Côte de Bréchain   ♈♈♈♈♈

Commune: Fyé. **Named vineyard:** Côte de Bréchain. **Area under production:** approximately 10 hectares. **Map:** page 136. An extension of Montée de Tonnerre lying along the valley of Bréchain. This excellent *climat* is marketed under the name of Montée de Tonnerre, of which it has practically all the same qualities, although it matures less satisfactorily.

Growers	Dauvissat, Michel 89800 Fyé	Fèvre, René 89800 Chablis
Bonnet, Maurice (Mme Veuve) 89800 Fyé	Droin, Jean-Paul 14 bis rue Jean Jaurès, 89800 Chablis	Grumet, Albert 3 rue de l'Hôpital, 89800 Chablis
Chapuis, Antoine 89800 Fyé	Fèvre, Régis 89800 Fyé	Mignard, Christian 40 rue Auxerroise, 89800 Chablis

Following his grandfather Georges and his father André, Christian Mignard is the loving proprietor of this little family estate whose vineyards cover six hectares in Bougros, Les Lys, and Vaillons ... and Bréchain (Montée de Tonnerre). He is as much a traditionalist as he is modest. But the quality of his production is remarkable.

Robin, Guy
13 rue Berthelot, 89800 Chablis

Servin (SCE)
20 av. d'Oberwesel, 89800 Chablis

Soupé, Michelle
32 rue d'Oberwesel, 89800 Chablis

Testut Frères (SCEA)
Ch. de Grenouille, 89800 Chablis

Vauroux (Domaine de)
89800 Chablis

Côte de Cuissy   ♟ ♟ ♟ ♟ ♟

Commune: Courgis. **Named vineyards:** Côte de Cuissy, Les Corvées, Bec d'Oiseau, Vallée de Cuissy. **Area under production:** approximately 9 hectares. **Map:** page 132. To the south-west of Courgis, Côte de Cuissy is a relatively recently recognized *climat* which can justly claim to be of good quality.

Marc Fillon's sign.

Growers

Adine, Christian
89800 Courgis

Chalmeau, Jacques
89530 Saint-Bris-le-Vineux

Colbois, Daniel
89530 Saint-Bris-le-Vineux

Dufour, Jean
Rue J. Ferrand, 89800 Courgis

Dufour, Robert
Rue J. Ferrand, 89800 Courgis

Fillon, Marc
53 rue B. Martin, 89530 Saint-Bris

Foulley, Jacques
89800 Courgis

Landais, Roger
89800 Courgis

Maingonnat, Raymond
89800 Courgis

Quittot, Gilbert
89800 Courgis

Race, Bernard
Rue J. Ferrand, 89800 Courgis

Rétif, Pierre
89800 Courgis

Côte de Fontenay   ♟ ♟ ♟ ♟ ♟

Commune: Fontenay-près-Chablis. **Named vineyards:** La Côte, Dine-Chien. **Area under production:** approximately 12 hectares. **Map:** page 134. On the right bank, favourably exposed to the south-east, the Côte de Fontenay is considered by some to rank among the top ranks of the *Premiers Crus*. They can certainly at times equal a Fourchaume in their finesse and the great delicacy of their bouquet.

Growers

Carré Frères (Pierre & Robert)
89800 Fontenay-près-Chablis

De Oliveira, Bernard
89800 Fontenay-près-Chablis

De Oliveira & Lecestre
89800 Fontenay-près-Chablis

De Oliveira Père & Fils (GAEC)
89800 Fontenay-près-Chablis

Fèvre Frères (GAEC)
89800 Fontenay-près-Chablis

Gautheron, Jean-Michel
89800 Fontenay-près-Chablis

Habert, Richard
89800 Fontenay-près-Chablis

Laroche (SCEA)
67 Grande Rue, 89800 Maligny

Mothe, Guy
89800 Fontenay-près-Chablis

Guy Mothe's vineyards are to be found on the Côte de Fontenay and at Vaucoupin. His wines are largely destined for the négociants *of Beaune, but you can always buy a few bottles direct from him. You will not regret it.*

Roy, Raymond & Claude
89800 Fontenay-près-Chablis

Vrignaud, Michel
89800 Fontenay-près-Chablis

143

Côte de Léchet

Commune: Milly. **Named vineyards:** Côte de Léchet, Le Château. **Area under production:** approximately 37 hectares. **Map:** page 135. Between Poinchy and Milly, this beautiful hillside is morphologically remarkable and is justifiably a *climat* in its own right. The situation and *terroir* of the Côte de Léchet rank it among the best *Premiers Crus* of the left bank.

The top of Côte de Léchet: the strict delimitation can be clearly seen.

Growers

Azo, Hervé
2 rue de Champlain, 89800 Chablis

Barat, Michel
89800 Milly

Boucheron, Robert
37 rue du Château, 89800 Chablis

Bourcey, Jean
89800 Milly

Bourcey, Roland
89800 Milly

Chatelain, Claude
89800 Poinchy

Chenevières (GAEC des)
89800 La Chapelle-Vaupelteigne

Coquard, Madeleine
89800 Poinchy

Coulaudin, Henri
89800 Milly

Dauvissat, Jean (SCEA)
89800 La Chapelle-Vaupelteigne

Dauvissat, René
8 rue Emile Zola, 89800 Chablis

Defaix, Bernard
17 rue du Château, 89800 Chablis

Defaix, Etienne
89800 Milly

Defaix, Jean
89800 Milly

Droin, Jean-Paul
14 bis rue Jean Jaurès, 89800 Chablis

Duchemin, Charles
89800 Poinchy

Fourrey, Jean-Jack
89800 Milly

Fourrey, Robert
89800 Milly

Guillaumont, Louis
89700 Tonnerre

Jannet, Jacqueline
89800 Poinchy

Jannet, Jean
89800 Milly

Malandes (Domaine des)
Rue Auxerroise, 89800 Chablis

Mignard, Marcel
89800 Milly

Morin, Jacques
89800 Poinchy

Mosnier, Sylvain
4 rue Derrière les Murs, 89800 Beine

Perreau, Martine
89800 Chablis

Perrot, Daniel
89800 Milly

Roblot, Cécilien
89800 Poinchy

Simonot, Louis
89800 Poinchy

Tremblay, Gérard
89800 Poinchy
Over ten years or so, this young viticulturalist has nearly tripled the 12 hectares he inherited from his fa- *ther. He has approximately 10 hectares of Premiers Crus in Montmains, Côte de Léchet, Côte de Træsmes, Fourchaume and L'Homme Mort. Combining a modern and traditional approach, he follows progress, at his own slow but steady pace. Vinification is carried out in temperature-controlled stainless steel vats, and hygiene is scrupulously observed. But ageing in wood is not ruled out, and the style of the firm is nicely balanced between classic rigour and that drinkability which appeals to mod-* *ern palates. Gérard Tremblay's dynamism has greatly expanded his foreign clientèle. His "Domaine des Isles" label is already well established in export markets, and deservedly so for its character and consistent quality; I am happy to endorse this reputation.*

Tremblay, Raymond
89800 Chablis

Villetard, Pierre
89800 Chablis

Côte de Savant ♟ ♟ ♟ ♟ ♟

Commune: Beine. **Named vineyards:** Côte de Savant, Frouquelin, Le Cotat Château, Le Verger. **Area under production:** approximately 21 hectares. **Map:** page 138. Facing south, the Côte de Savant stretches along the road from Beine to Chablis. This excellent aspect and the Kimmeridgian *terroir* yield good wine with a classic character.

Growers

Ballantier, Alfred
La Haute Route, 10290 Marcilly

Bethery, Daniel
4 Moulin du Faubourg, Chablis

Bonnet, Jean-Marie (SCEA)
14 rue Jules Rathier, 89800 Chablis

Bouchard, Pascal
17 bd Lamarque, 89800 Chablis

Cartaut, Adrien
23 rue du Ruisseau, 89800 Beine

De l'Orme à Véron (SCA)
89800 Lignorelles

Du Parc (Verret & Fils)
7 rte de Champs, 89530 Saint-Bris

Geoffroy, Alain
4 rue de l'Equerre, 89800 Beine

Hamelin, Marc (Domaine)
89800 Lignorelles

Michaut Frères (GAEC)
41 rue du Ruisseau, 89800 Beine

Naulin, Jean-Marie
6 rue du Carouge, 89800 Beine

Naulin, Robert
6 rue du Carouge, 89800 Beine

Patrice, André
5 ruelle du Grand Jour, 89800 Beine

Roblot, Daniel
Rue Porte d'Auxerre, 89800 Beine

Villain, Robert
8 chemin des Fossés, 89800 Beine

Côte des Près Girots ♟ ♟ ♟ ♟ ♟

Commune: Fleys. **Named vineyards:** Côte des Près Girots, La Côte, Sur la Côte. **Area under production:** approximately 7 hectares. **Map:** page 137. This is the most easterly of the *Premiers Crus*, lying immediately north of the village of Fleys along the road from Chablis to Tonnerre. It enjoys a very favourable southern aspect and its potential vineyard area gives it an appreciable production capacity. Its name deserves to be better known.

Growers

Barat, Michel
89800 Milly

Carré Frères (Pierre & Robert)
89800 Fontenay-près-Chablis

Dauvissat, Jean-Claude
2 Grande Rue, 89800 Beine

Gautheron, Jean
89800 Fleys

Laroche, Roger
89800 Fleys

Nicolle, Paul
89800 Chablis

Nicolle, Robert
89800 Fleys

Philippon, Louis & André
89800 Fleys

Rousseau, Robert
89800 Fleys

Côte de Vaubarousse ♀♀♀♀♀

Commune: Fyé. **Named vineyard:** Côte de Vaubarousse. **Area under production:** approximately 2 hectares. **Map:** page 136. Within the small area of the vineyards of Fyé (a commune which is today linked to Chablis), the slopes of Vaubarousse extend to the south-east of Berdiot. A very small *climat* which is not marketed under its own name, it can produce wine of a quality quite worthy of interest in its own right.

| Growers | Bonnet, Marcel
89800 Fyé | Fèvre, Régis
89800 Fyé |

Forêt ♀♀♀♀♀

Commune: Chablis. **Named vineyard:** Les Forêts. **Area under production:** approximately 21 hectares. **Map:** page 133. In two sections, being separated by a part of Les Butteaux, the *climat* of Forêt (or "Les Forêts") is one of the best on the left bank. It has the advantage of being relatively well known to the general public and its fine reputation is generally justified, although, like its neighbours, it is particularly susceptible to the effects of cold and wet years.

Growers	Dieux, Jacques Chemin la Vieille Voye, Chablis	Michel, Louis (& Fils) 11 bd des Ferrières, 89800 Chablis
Besson, Alain 19 rue Emile Zola, 89800 Chablis	Drouhin, Joseph 1 rue d'Enfer, 21200 Beaune	Moreau, René 5 rue des Fossés, 89800 Chablis
Collet, Claude 10 rue A. Hovelacque, 89800 Chablis	Duplessis Père & Fils 5 quai de Reugny, 89800 Chablis	Pinson (SCEA du Domaine) 5 quai Voltaire, 89800 Chablis
Dauvissat, René 8 rue Emile Zola, 89800 Chablis *Dauvissat's "Forêt" is undoubtedly one of the best bottles to be drunk from this Premier Cru. It is to be found in several great Paris restaurants, notably in Martin Cantegrit's excellent Récamier. René Dauvissat's grandfather was a cooper by profession but he loved his little vineyard. Following family tradition, the Dauvissat wines are aged in wood which imparts a classic balance, firm bouquet and excellent ageing potential.*	Feuillebois, Jean 13 rue de Reugny, 89800 Chablis Grumet, Andrée 3 rue de l'Hôpital, 89800 Chablis Hamelin, Marc (Domaine) 89800 Lignorelles Maladière (Domaine de la) 14 rue Jules Rathier, 89800 Chablis Martin, Jean-Claude Rue Jacques Ferrand, 89800 Courgis	Race, Denis 16 rue de Chichée, 89800 Chablis Raveneau, François 9 rue de Chichée, 89800 Chablis Tremblay, Louis 89800 La Chapelle-Vaupelteigne Vocoret, R. (& Fils) 16 rue Emile Zola, 89800 Chablis

Fourchaume ♀♀♀♀♀

Commune: La Chapelle-Vaupelteigne. **Named vineyard:** Fourchaume. **Area under production:** approximately 34 hectares. **Map:** page 134. Without any shadow of doubt, Fourchaume is one the *grands seigneurs* among the *Premiers Crus*, and its worldwide reputation justifies its taking a certain number of neighbouring estates under its wing. The

146

climat of Fourchaume is an extension of the northerly slopes of the *Grands Crus*, and the wines it produces thus often share the qualities of these . A great, true Fourchaume can be distinguished by its power and breeding and its bouquet, which can be extraordinary.

Growers

Azo, Hervé
2 rue de Champlain, 89800 Chablis

Bérilley, Roland
89800 Fontenay-près-Chablis

Bouchard, Pascal
17 bd Lamarque, 89800 Chablis
Pascal Bouchard was "imported" to Chablis from Ligny-le-Châtel by his marriage to Joëlle Tremblay. There are no more deeply-rooted viticulturalists than the Tremblays. This young couple took on the family estate in 1979 and today have about 20 hectares under production, of which

Madame Joëlle Bouchard

one is in the Grand Cru *"Les Clos" and another in Fourchaume. The rest of their* Premier Cru *land is in Mont de Milieu, Montmains and Beauroy. The Chablis AOC land under their control covers approximately eleven hectares and that of Petit-Chablis one hectare. This distribution is highly judicious, affording a good range yet keeping the undertaking within manageable proportions. It is clear that together the Bouchards make a good team. Pascal keep an eye on everything and runs his vineyards and his cellar with equal proficiency. Joëlle is a notable linguist and travels all over northern Europe by plane and car. The whole of their produce is marketed by themselves. All their wines are bottled on site. The style is "fresh, delicate, fruity" and is soon ready for drinking. It is very satisfactory all round. What a pity for the French that all their production goes for export!*

Boudin, A. (GAEC Chanteme)
89800 Chablis

Boudin, Francis
89800 La Chapelle-Vaupelteigne

Bourcey, Roland
89800 Milly

Carré Frères (Pierre & Robert)
89800 Fontenay-près-Chablis

Chatelain, André
89800 Poinchy

Chatelain, Claude
89800 Poinchy

Chenevières (GAEC des)
89800 La Chapelle-Vaupelteigne

Crochot, Armand
89800 La Chapelle-Vaupelteigne

Dauvissat, Jean (SCEA)
89800 La Chapelle-Vaupelteigne

Defert, René
89800 Ligny-le-Châtel

Droin, Jean-Paul
14 bis rue Jean Jaurès, 89800 Chablis

Dupas, Henri
89800 Fontenay-près-Chablis

Duplessis Père & Fils
5 quai de Reugny, 89800 Chablis

Fèvre Frères (GAEC)
89800 Fontenay-près-Chablis

Fèvre, Régis
89800 Fyé

Geoffroy, Alain
4 rue de l'Equerre, 89800 Beine

Goulley, Jean
89800 La Chapelle-Vaupelteigne

Jannet, Jean
89800 Milly

La Fourchaume (GAEC de)
89800 La Chapelle-Vaupelteigne
Francis and Jacques Philippon are brothers and work together on their vines, which are immaculately tended. They are proprietors at Fourchaume, Montmains and Vaillons, producing sinewy, sappy wines which are highly esteemed by the négociant trade. They keep back a part of their harvest for a number of faithful private customers, who must certainly not be disappointed by the quality of wines they receive.

Laroche (SCEA)
67 Grande Rue, 89800 Maligny

Lordou, René
89800 Fontenay-près-Chablis

Malandes (Domaine des)
61 rue Auxerroise, 89800 Chablis
This young viticulturalist, Lyne Tremblay, comes from a long line of growers in the region, and is not afraid to run her estate of some 20 hectares by herself. The Domaine Rottiers-Clotilde has been renamed Domaine des Malandes, and she now runs it with her husband Jean-Bernard Marchive.
Their vines are spread out among the good crus *of Chablis:* Grand Cru *Vaudésir,* Premiers Crus *Montmains, Fourchaume, Côte de Léchet and Vaux de Vey, together with a proportion of Chablis AOC, and 75% of this excellent production goes for export. The rest is kept for up-market restaurants and faithful private customers.*

Porcheron, Ulysse
89800 Fontenay-près-Chablis

Race, Jacques
89800 Chablis

Race, Monique
89800 Chablis

Rousseau, Jean-Pierre
89800 Chablis

Rutem, Maurice
89800 Chablis

Simonot, Rémy
27 rue de Poinchy, 89800 Chablis

Thouveray, Patrick
89800 La Chapelle-Vaupelteigne

Tremblay, André
89800 La Chapelle-Vaupelteigne

Tremblay, Gérard
89800 Poinchy

Tremblay, Jacques
89800 La Chapelle-Vaupelteigne
With about 7 hectares of vines, of which 1.5 are at Fourchaume, Jacques Tremblay is a "big small producer" who sells the main part of his yearly output in bulk to the négociants. For the few thousand bottles he keeps back for direct sales, he favours early bottling so as to retain maximum freshness and fruit.

Tremblay, Louis
89800 La Chapelle-Vaupelteigne

Tupinier, Daniel
89800 La Chapelle-Vaupelteigne

147

Les Beauregards ♟♟♟♟♟

Commune: Courgis. **Named vineyards:** Les Beauregards, Hauts des Chambres du Roi. **Area under production:** approximately 21 hectares. **Map:** page 132. This *climat* extends as far as the Côte de Cuissy to the south-west, and is the furthest away from the village of Chablis. It is rather out on a limb geographically in relation to the heart of the Chablis vignoble but this is compensated for by an excellent aspect, ensuring maximum sunshine.

Grower
Martin, Jean-Claude Rue J. Ferrand, 89800 Courgis

Les Epinottes ♟♟♟♟♟

Commune: Chablis. **Named vineyard:** Les Epinottes. **Area under production:** approximately 22 hectares. **Map:** page 133. Very little known by the public because it is rarely marketed under its own name, this *Premier Cru* is nevertheless a very good *climat* on the left bank, capable of producing wine of a superior quality.

Growers

Bègue, Jean
11 rue Jules Rathier, 89800 Chablis

Bichot, Albert
11 bd Joffre, 21200 Beaune

Château de Viviers (Lupé-Cholet)
89800 Viviers
With vineyards in Les Epinottes and Vaucoupin, Château de Viviers has all its wines handled today by the respected Burgundy firm of Lupé-Cholet at Nuits-Saint-Georges. The principal vineyard area is in Viviers, in the Chablis AOC. But the Premier Cru Chablis, very limited in quantity, is widely appreciated for its distinctive style, reinforced by a firm attack.

Collet, Jean (& Fils)
1 rue du Panonceau, 89800 Chablis

Dauvissat, René
8 rue Emile Zola, 89800 Chablis

Droin Père & Fils (GAEC)
3 rue de Montmain, 89800 Chablis

Drouhin, Joseph
1 rue d'Enfer, 21200 Beaune

Feuillebois, Jean-Claude
6 rue de Montmain, 89800 Chablis

Gautherin, Alain
6 bd Lamarque, 89800 Chablis

Gautherin, Raoul
6 bd Lamarque, 89800 Chablis

Grumet, Albert
3 rue de l'Hôpital, 89800 Chablis

Jacquin, Jean
30 rue de Chichée, 89800 Chablis

Laroche (SCEA)
67 Grande Rue, 89800 Maligny

Long Depaquit, Albert (GFA)
45 rue Auxerroise, 89800 Chablis

Mignard, Christian
40 rue Auxerroise, 89800 Chablis

Moreau, Jean (Domaines)
Rue Auxerroise, 89800 Chablis

Robin, Alain
24 bis rue Jean Jaurès, 89800 Chablis

Robin, Michel
2 rue du Puits, 89800 Chablis

Rogié, André
Chemin des Petits Dieux, Chablis

Rogié, François
Clos des Dieux, 89800 Chablis

Servin (SCE)
20 av. d'Oberwesel, 89800 Chablis

Vocoret, R. (& Fils)
16 rue Emile Zola, 89800 Chablis

Les Fourneaux ♈♈♈♈♈

Commune: Fleys. **Named vineyard:** Les Fourneaux. **Area under production:** approximately 2 hectares. **Map:** page 137. This is one of the three *Premiers Crus* situated in the commune of Fleys. With a good high exposure towards the south-east, the little *climat* of Les Fourneaux produces wines which can mature well, but never lose a suggestion of hardness.

Growers	Lecullier, René (Mme) 89800 Fleys	Philippon, Louis & André 89800 Fleys
Barat, Michel 89800 Milly	**Lesage, René (Mme)** 89800 Chablis	
Gautheron, Jean 89800 Fleys	**Nicolle, Paul** 89800 Chablis	

Les Landes et Verjuts ♈♈♈♈♈

Commune: Courgis. **Named vineyard:** Les Landes et Verjuts. **Area under production:** approximately 6 hectares. **Map:** page 132. Immediately to the north of Courgis, this *Premier Cru* is a relatively recent one and cannot claim to rival the best, being content with a very reasonable standard of quality.

Growers	Colbois, Daniel 89530 Saint-Bris-le-Vineux	Legland, Bernard 89800 Préhy
Chalmeau, Jacques 89530 Saint-Bris-le-Vineux	**Colbois, Michel** 89530 Saint-Bris-le-Vineux	**Race, Bernard** Rue Jacques Ferrand, 89800 Courgis
Chapotin, Philibert 89800 Courgis	**Foulley, Philippe** Rue J. Ferrand, 89800 Courgis	**Rétif, Pierre** 89800 Courgis

Les Lys ♈♈♈♈♈

Commune: Chablis. **Named vineyards:** Champlain, Les Lys. **Area under production:** approximately 12 hectares. **Map:** page 133. A "historic" *Premier Cru* if ever there was one, for this area belonged to the crown under the Ancien Régime, as its name testifies. Les Lys is to the south of Milly and lies quite close to the village of Chablis. In great years, this *climat* can reach the highest peaks of finesse. The name is relatively well known to the public and enjoys a well deserved reputation.

Growers	Defaix, Daniel 89800 Milly	Feuillebois, René 6 rue de Montmain, 89800 Chablis
Bourcey, Roland 89800 Milly	**Defaix, Jean** 89800 Milly	**Filippi, Jeanne-Paule (SC)** 14 rue Jules Rathier, 89800 Chablis
Defaix, Bernard 17 rue du Château, 89800 Chablis	**Defaix, Etienne** 89800 Milly	**Gautherin, André** 24 av. Jean Jaurès, 89800 Chablis

149

Gautherin, Raoul 6 bd Lamarque, 89800 Chablis	Maladière (Domaine de la) 14 rue Jules Rathier, 89800 Chablis	Villetard, Pierre 15 rue de Léchet, 89800 Chablis
Jannet, Jean 89800 Milly	Mignard, Christian 40 rue Auxerroise, 89800 Chablis	
Long Depaquit, Albert (GFA) 45 rue Auxerroise, 89800 Chablis	Raoult, Eliane Vezannes, 89700 Tonnerre	

L'Homme Mort ♙♙♙♙♙

Commune: Maligny. **Named vineyards:** L'Homme Mort, La Grande Côte, Bois Seguin, L'Ardillier. **Area under production:** approximately 40 hectares. **Map:** page 134. It is perhaps the macabre associations of the name which tend to make growers here prefer to give their wine the Fourchaume appellation, which is also more prestigious. The wine can be of excellent quality.

Growers	Gautheron, Emile Rue Auxerroise, 89800 Chablis	Seguinot, Daniel 89800 Maligny
Baillard, (SCEA du Domaine) 20 av. d'Oberwesel, 89800 Chablis	Goulley, Jean 89800 La Chapelle-Vaupelteigne	Seguinot, Roger 4 rue de Méré, 89800 Maligny
Chantemerle (GAEC) 89800 La Chapelle-Vaupelteigne *If you want to find a bottle of Premier Cru Chablis whose label bears the words "L'Homme Mort", there is only one address: that of Adhémar Boudin at La Chapelle-Vaupelteigne. He is the only producer in this very respectable climat not to give his wines the name of Fourchaume. All the wines of the Chantemerle firm, under the enlightened direction of Adhémar Boudin, are more often than not impressive, from the Petit-Chablis to the Premier Cru. He is a grower of the old school, and all the work, both in the vines and in the cellar, is directed by Madame la Lune. To judge by the results, she is an excellent supervisor.*	Jolly, Henri 2 rue Auxerroise, 89800 Maligny	Thouveray, Patrick 89800 La Chapelle-Vaupelteigne
	Jolly, Paul 89800 Maligny	Tremblay, Gérard 89800 Poinchy
	La Fourchaume (GAEC de) 89800 La Chapelle-Vaupelteigne	Tremblay, Louis 89800 La Chapelle-Vaupelteigne
	Laroche (SCEA) 67 Grande Rue, 89800 Maligny	Vocoret, Maurice 89800 Maligny
	Laroche, Patrick 1 rue des Ecoles, 89800 Maligny	Vocoret, Yvon 5 rue Chanteprime, 89800 Maligny
	Lasnier, Pierre 19 rue de Chanteprime, Maligny	
	Lorot, Max 66 Grande Rue, 89800 Maligny	
Chenevières (GAEC des) 89800 La Chapelle-Vaupelteigne	Pautre Père & Fils (GAEC) 89800 Lignorelles	
Dalannoy, Philippe 89800 Chablis	Rousseau, Jean-Pierre 89800 Chablis	
Dauvissat, Jean (SCEA) 89800 La Chapelle-Vaupelteigne	Rutem, Maurice 89800 Chablis	
Durup, Jean Dne de l'Eglantière, 89800 Chablis	Savary, Olivier 89800 Maligny	

Mélinots ♙♙♙♙♙

Commune: Chablis. **Named vineyard:** Les Minos. **Area under production:** approximately 10 hectares. **Map:** page 133. This is a typical example of how names marry and change. Mélinots comes from the name of the place known as "Les Minos", which is directly opposite, Les Lys on the same hillside as Roncières, Vaillons, etc. It appears that this excellent *Premier Cru* is not marketed under its own name.

Growers

Bègue, Charles
12 rue de Chitry, 89800 Chablis

Besson, Félix
28 rue de Reugny, 89800 Chablis

Billaud, Jean (SCEA)
1 quai de Reugny, 89800 Chablis

Collet, Jean (& Fils)
1 rue du Panonceau, 89800 Chablis

Dauvissat, Jean
89800 Chablis

Defaix, Etienne
89800 Milly

Duplessis Père & Fils
5 quai de Reugny, 89800 Chablis

Feuillebois, René
6 rue de Montmain, 89800 Chablis

Gautherin, Raoul
6 bd Lamarque, 89800 Chablis

Grumet, Albert
3 rue de l'Hôpital, 89800 Chablis

Grumet, André
25 rue Hovelacque, 89800 Chablis

Long Depaquit, Albert (GFA)
45 rue Auxerroise, 89800 Chablis

Maladière (Domaine de la)
14 rue Jules Rathier, 89800 Chablis

Robin, Alain
24 bis rue Jean Jaurès, 89800 Chablis

Robin, Guy
13 rue Berthelot, 89800 Chablis

Mont de Milieu   ♟ ♟ ♟ ♟ ♟

Communes: Fleys, Fyé. **Named vineyards:** Mont de Milieu, Vallée de Chigot. **Area under production:** approximately 34 hectares. **Map:** page 136. This distinguished *Premier Cru* enjoys a geographical situation comparable in every way with that of the *Grands Crus* and faces south-south-east, so guaranteeing good mean temperatures and a particularly high number of hours of sunshine. Mont de Milieu is undoubtedly one of the three best *climats* among the *Premiers Crus*.

Growers

Aufrere, Dominique
89800 Fleys

Barat, Michel
89800 Milly

Besson, Félix
28 rue de Reugny, 89800 Chablis

Billaud-Simon & Fils
1 quai de Reugny, 89800 Chablis
Proprietors at Les Clos and Vaudésir and, in the Grands Crus, at Preuses and Blanchot. In the Premiers Crus, they are to be found at Montée de Tonnerre and Vaillons. They market their production partly through local négociants and partly by direct sales, notably to the U.S.A. The style of the wine is the result of a fine balance between the old and the new: brilliant and perfumed, with bite and a certain severity.

Bocquet, Henri
89700 Tonnerre

Bouchard, Pascal
17 bd Lamarque, 89800 Chablis

Collet, Jean (& Fils)
1 rue du Panonceau, 89800 Chablis

Couperot, Alain
89800 Fleys

Dauvissat, Jean
89800 Chablis

Dauvissat, Lionel
89800 Fleys

Drouhin, Joseph (SA)
7 rue d'Enfer, 21200 Beaune

Feuillebois, Jean
13 rue de Reugny, 89800 Chablis

Foulley, Albert
89800 Fleys

Fournillon, Bernard
89800 Chablis

Fourrey, Jean-Jack
89800 Milly

Gautherin, Raoul
6 bd Lamarque, 89800 Chablis

Gautheron, Jean
89800 Fleys

Gouailhardou, Jean-Pierre
18 rue Auxerroise, 89800 Chablis

Goulley, Jean
89800 La Chapelle-Vaupelteigne

Grossot, Jean-Pierre
89800 Fleys

Laffay, Thierry
5 rue du Panonceau, 89800 Chablis

Laroche, Claude
89800 Chablis

Laroche, Roger
89800 Fleys

Lavens, Jean-Mary
Chemin du Moulin, 89800 Chablis

Lavens, Michel
45 HLM Les Picards, 89800 Chablis

Lecullier, René
89800 Fleys

Lesage, Paulette
89800 Fleys

Lesage, René
89800 Chablis

Michaut, André
89800 Fleys

Michaut, Daniel
89800 Fleys

Michaut, Michel
89800 Chichée

Michel, Maurice
9 rue Emile Zola, 89800 Chablis

Nicolle, Paul
89800 Chablis

Nicolle, Robert
89800 Fleys

Philippon, André
89800 Fleys
As proprietor in Mont de Milieu and in the Chablis AOC, André Philippon is an independent viticulturalist who has staked his all on a private clientele. He himself markets three-quarters of his production in bottle, the rest being sold in bulk to négociants. Vinifying in stainless steel vats, he strives for maximum fruit flavour. Reliable, worth-while buys for the lover of fine wines.

Philippon, Louis & André
89800 Fleys

151

Louis Pinson

Pinson, Louis
2 rue Vieilles Boucheries, Chablis
The Pinsons are a very old Chablis family who have been growers from

father to son. Their little estate is split up over different good climats such as Mont de Milieu, Forêt, Montmains and Montée de Tonnerre. The wines are reliable, in traditional style and more often than not are well-suited to ageing.

Pinson (SCEA du Domaine)
5 quai Voltaire, 89800 Chablis

Poupion, Robert
89800 Fleys

Race, Suzanne
14 rue de Chichée, 89800 Chablis

Rousseau, Robert
89800 Fleys

Simon, Christian
24 av. Jean Jaurès, 89800 Chablis

Vocoret, Patrice
15 rue du Panonceau, 89800 Chablis

Vocoret R. (& Fils)
16 rue Emile Zola, 89800 Chablis

Montée de Tonnerre   ♉♉♉♉♉

Commune: Fyé. **Named vineyard:** Montée de Tonnerre. **Area under production:** approximately 6 hectares. **Map:** page 136. Montée de Tonnerre and Mont de Milieu are equally excellent. Although considerably smaller than its great rival, Montée de Tonnerre has succeeded in "colonizing" Chapelot, Pied d'Aloue and Côte de Bréchain. If these assimilations sometimes seem rather unsporting, in this case, it is a question of one and the same *climat* in the broad sense of the term. Each of the four localities produces the same level of quality: superb.

Growers	**Fèvre, René** 89800 Chablis	**Simon, Christian** 24 av. Jean Jaurès, 89800 Chablis
Billaud, Jean & André 1 quai de Reugny, 89800 Chablis	**Robert, Albert** 24 rue Jean Jaurès, 89800 Chablis	**Vocoret, R. (& Fils)** 16 rue Emile Zola, 89800 Chablis
Droin, Jean-Paul 14 bis rue Jean Jaurès, 89800 Chablis	**Robin, Alain** 24 bis rue Jean Jaurès, 89800 Chablis	
Fenice, Paule 17 rue P. Bert, 94130 Saint-Mandé	**Servin (SCE)** 20 av. d'Oberwesel, 89800 Chablis	

Montmains   ♉♉♉♉♉

Commune: Chablis. **Named vineyard:** Les Monts Mains. **Area under production:** approximately 37 hectares. **Map:** page 133. Stretching away from Forêt to the north-east, Montmains has a more than honourable place on the recommended list of *Premiers Crus* from the left bank. The wines produced here have a certain initial severity which makes them ideally suitable for ageing.

Growers	**Collet, Claude** 10 rue A. Hovelacque, 89800 Chablis	**Dauvissat, Jean (SCEA)** 89800 La Chapelle-Vaupelteigne
Besson, Félix 28 rue de Reugny, 89800 Chablis	**Collet, Gilles** 1 rue du Panonceau, 89800 Chablis	**Droin, Jean-Paul** 14 bis rue Jean Jaurès, 89800 Chablis
Bouchard, Pascal 17 bd Lamarque, 89800 Chablis	**Collet, Jean (& Fils)** 1 rue du Panonceau, 89800 Chablis	**Droin, René** 8 rue du Panonceau, 89800 Chablis
Chapotin, Jean-Pierre Rue J. Rousseau, 89800 Courgis	**Dauvissat, Jean** 89800 Chablis	**Drouhin, Joseph** 1 rue d'Enfer, 21200 Beaune

Duplessis, Marcel (& Fils)
5 quai de Reugny, 89800 Chablis
Owns several parcels in Montée de Tonnerre, Montmains, Fourchaume and Vaillons, together with nearly an acre in Les Clos: about 5 hectares in all. His wines really are vinified and aged in traditional style: six months in the vat and a year in wood. The results are very satisfactory.

Durup, Jean
Dne de l'Eglantière, 89800 Chablis

Feuillebois, Jean
13 rue de Reugny, 89800 Chablis

Feuillebois, Jean-Claude
6 rue de Montmain, 89800 Chablis

Feuillebois, René
6 rue de Montmain, 89800 Chablis

Gautherin, Gérard
2 rue Robert Schuman, Chablis

Gautherin, Raoul
6 bd Lamarque, 89800 Chablis

Gouailhardou, Jean-Pierre
18 rue Auxerroise, 89800 Chablis

Goulley, Jean
89800 La Chapelle-Vaupelteigne

Grumet, André
25 rue A. Hovelacque, 89800 Chablis

Jacquin, Jean
30 rue de Chichée, 89800 Chablis

La Fourchaume (GAEC de)
89800 La Chapelle-Vaupelteigne

Laroche (SCEA)
67 Grande Rue, 89800 Maligny

Laroche, Roger
89800 Fleys

Montmains and Roncières in autumn's glory

Lavens, Michel
45 HLM Les Picards, 89800 Chablis

Maladière (Domaine de la)
14 rue Jules Rathier, 89800 Chablis

Malandes (Domaine des)
Rue Auxerroise, 89800 Chablis

Michel, Louis (& Fils)
11 bd des Ferrières, 89800 Chablis

Michel, Maurice
9 rue Emile Zola, 89800 Chablis

Moreau, Roger
5 rue des Fossés, 89800 Chablis

Robin, Guy
13 rue Berthelot, 89800 Chablis

Robin, Michel
2 rue du Puits, 89000 Chablis

Pinson (SCEA du Domaine)
5 quai Voltaire, 89800 Chablis

Simon, Christian
24 av. Jean Jaurès, 89800 Chablis

Simon, Jules
24 av. Jean Jaurès, 89800 Chablis

Testut Frères (SCEA)
Ch. de Grenouille, 89800 Chablis

Tremblay, Gérard
89800 Poinchy

Tremblay, Louis
89800 La Chapelle-Vaupelteigne

Tremblay, Raymond
89800 Chablis

Tricon, Olivier
8 rue Marcelin Berthelot, Chablis

Vocoret, R. (& Fils)
16 rue Emile Zola, 89800 Chablis

Morein ♟♟♟♟♟

Commune: Fleys. **Named vineyard:** Morein. **Area under production:** approximately 5 hectares. **Map:** page 137. On excellent vine-growing land, the little *climat* of Morein, lying to the north-west of the village of Fleys, follows on from Les Fourneaux. It can be considered as a good standby *Premier Cru.*

Growers	Drouhin, Joseph (SA) 7 rue d'Enfer, 21200 Beaune	Rousseau, Robert 89800 Fleys
Dauvissat, Jean-Claude 2 Grande Rue, 89800 Beine	Fournillon, Bernard 89800 Fleys	
Dauvissat, Lionel 89800 Fleys	Gautheron, Jean 89800 Fleys	

Pied d'Aloue ♀♀♀♀♀

Commune: Fyé. **Named vineyards:** Pied d'Aloue, Sous Pied d'Aloue. **Area under production:** approximately 7 hectares. **Map:** page 136. Do not expect to find this name on any label, but put your trust in the producer in this *climat,* who offers you "his" Montée de Tonnerre.

Growers	Filippi, Jeanne-Paule (SC) 14 rue Jules Rathier, 89800 Chablis	Servin (SCE) 20 av. d'Oberwesel, 89800 Chablis
Billaud, Jean & André 1 quai de Reugny, 89800 Chablis	Raveneau, François 9 rue de Chichée, 89800 Chablis	Soupé, Michelle 32 rue d'Oberwesel, 89800 Chablis
Duplessis Père & Fils 5 quai de Reugny, 89800 Chablis	Robin, Guy 13 rue Berthelot, 89800 Chablis	Vocoret, R. (& Fils) 16 rue Emile Zola, 89800 Chablis

Roncières ♀♀♀♀♀

Commune: Chablis. **Named vineyard:** Les Roncières. **Area under production:** approximately 19 hectares. **Map:** page 133. This micro-*climat* lies on the extensive south-western slopes of Chablis, where Beugnons, Châtains, Mélinots, Vaillons, etc. are also to be found. In practice, it is possible to confuse it with Vaillons, and, in terms of quality, the comparaison is not unfavourabled.

Growers	Feuillebois, René 6 rue de Montmain, 89800 Chablis	Simon, Christian 24 av. Jean Jaurès, 89800 Chablis
Bègue, Charles 12 rue de Chitry, 89800 Chablis	Grumet, André 25 rue A. Hovelacque, 89800 Chablis	Soupé, Michelle 32 rue d'Oberwesel, 89800 Chablis
Bègue, Jean 11 rue Jules Rathier, 89800 Chablis	Laffay, Thierry 5 rue du Panonceau, 89800 Chablis	Testut Frères (SCEA) Ch. de Grenouille, 89800 Chablis
Bègue, Maurice 6 rue A. Hovelacque, 89800 Chablis	Laroche (SCEA) 67 Grande Rue, 89800 Maligny	Vocoret, R. (& Fils) 16 rue Emile Zola, 89800 Chablis
Boucherat, Guy 12 allée des Fleurs, 89800 Chablis	Michel, Louis (& Fils) 11 bd des Ferrières, 89800 Chablis	
Collet, Claude 10 rue A. Hovelacque, 89800 Chablis	Moreau, Jean (Domaines) Rue Auxerroise, 89800 Chablis	
Collet, Jean (& Fils) 1 rue du Panonceau, 89800 Chablis	Moreau, Roger 5 rue des Fossés, 89800 Chablis	
Droin Père & Fils (GAEC) 3 rue de Montmain, 89800 Chablis	Race, Suzanne 14 rue de Chichée, 89800 Chablis	
Drouhin, Joseph 1 rue d'Enfer, 21200 Beaune	Servin (SCE) 20 av. d'Oberwesel, 89800 Chablis	

Sécher �♀♀♀♀♀

Commune: Chablis. **Named vineyard:** Sécher. **Area under production:** approximately 11 hectares. **Map:** page 133. (See also Roncières.) Sécher rather resembles Les Lys, which is its neighbours. The name is virtually unknown the market but the *terroir* is good.

Growers

Billaud, Jean & André
1 quai de Reugny, 89800 Chablis

Collet, Jean (& Fils)
1 rue du Panonceau, 89800 Chablis

Defaix, Bernard
17 rue du Château, 89800 Chablis

Defaix, Etienne
89800 Milly

Droin Père & Fils (GAEC)
3 rue de Montmain, 89800 Chablis

Drouhin, Joseph (SA)
7 rue d'Enfer, 21200 Beaune

Drouhin, Joseph
1 rue d'Enfer, 21200 Beaune

Feuillebois, René
13 rue de Reugny, 89800 Chablis

Gautherin, Raoul
6 bd Lamarque, 89800 Chablis

Jacquin, Jean
30 rue de Chichée, 89800 Chablis

Laroche (SCEA)
67 Grande Rue, 89800 Maligny

Michel, Louis (& Fils)
11 bd des Ferrières, 89800 Chablis

Mignard, Christian
40 rue Auxerroise, 89800 Chablis

Moreau, Roger
5 rue des Fossés, 89800 Chablis

Robin, Albert
24 rue Jean Jaurès, 89800 Chablis

Robin, Marie-Claire
Moulin du Faubourg, 89800 Chablis

Servin (SCE)
20 av. d'Oberwesel, 89800 Chablis

Vocoret, R. (& Fils)
16 rue Emile Zola, 89800 Chablis

Trœsmes ♀♀♀♀♀

Commune: Beine. **Named vineyards:** Côte de Trœsmes, Adroit de Vau Renard. **Area under production:** approximately 16 hectares. **Map:** page 135. Trœsmes (or Troêmes, or any other similar spelling) is one of the best *Premiers Crus* on the left bank, especially the vineyards closest to the village of Poinchy. It is an even slope, differentiated within itself only by the variety of exposures. Trœsmes is characterized by its extreme finesse – the finest of all, perhaps.

Growers

Chatelain, Claude
89800 Poinchy

Coquard, Madeleine
89800 Poinchy

Droin, René
8 rue du Panonceau, 89800 Chablis

Du Parc (Verret & Fils)
7 rte de Champs, 89530 Saint-Bris-le-Vineux

Geoffroy, Alain
4 rue de l'Equerre, 89800 Beine
The mayor of Beine who, as such, manned the barricades at the time of the last delimitation revision by the I.N.A.O. He has some 25 hectares in the area and is resolutely modern in his approach to vinification. His

wines are "fresh, light and fruity" in style, differing from more traditional Chablis in the rapidity with which they are ready for drinking.

Grossot, Jean-Pierre
89800 Fleys

Lhoste, Maurice
89800 La Chapelle-Vaupelteigne

Magarian, Gulbeng
89800 Poinchy

Maladière (Domaine de la)
14 rue Jules Rathier, 89800 Chablis

Michaut Frères (GAEC)
41 rue du Ruisseau, 89800 Beine
Bernard and Jean Michaut have the largest harvest return figures in the commune of Beine. They take the whole of their harvest to the cave coopérative.

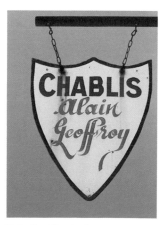

Alain Geoffroy's sign.

155

Morin, Georges 1 rue de Beine, 89800 Chablis	**Simonot, Louis** 89800 Poinchy	**Tremblay, Suzanne** 89800 Lignorelles
Morin, Jacques 89800 Poinchy	**Simonot, Rémy** 27 rue de Poinchy, 89800 Chablis	**Villain (GAEC)** 11 rue de la Mairie, 89800 Beine
Mosnier, Sylvain 4 rue Derrière les Murs, 89800 Beine	**Tremblay, Gérard** 89800 Poinchy	

Vaillons   ♀♀♀♀♀

Commune: Chablis. **Named vineyards:** Les Vaillons, Sur les Vaillons. **Area under production:** approximately 15 hectares. **Map:** page 133. Vaillons is a justifiably famous *climat*. It lies in the centre of the great hillside to the south-west of Chablis and it sets the example for all its neighbours. Its wines are generous, of great substance and incisive. They "fill the mouth". In certain good years they may even be confused with Fourchaume.

Growers	**Coulaudin, Henri** 89800 Milly	**Moreau, Jean (Domaines)** Rue Auxerroise, 89800 Chablis
Auffray (Ancien Domaine) 14 rue Jules Rathier, 89800 Chablis	**Dauvissat, Jean** 89800 Chablis	**Race, Suzanne** 14 rue de Chichée, 89800 Chablis
Barat, Bernard 89800 Milly	**Defaix, Bernard** 17 rue du Château, 89800 Chablis	**Raveneau, Jean-Marie** 9 rue de Chichée, 89800 Chablis
Barat, Michel 89800 Milly	**Defaix, Daniel** 89800 Milly	**Robin, Denis** 89800 Chablis
Bègue, Jean 11 rue Jules Rathier, 89800 Chablis	**Droin, Jean-Paul** 14 bis rue Jean Jaurès, 89800 Chablis	**Robin, Marie-Claire** Moulin du Faubourg, 89800 Chablis
Besson, Felix 28 rue de Reugny, 89800 Chablis	**Filippi, Jeanne-Paule (SC)** 14 rue Jules Rathier, 89800 Chablis	**Servin (SCE)** 20 av. d'Oberwesel, 89800 Chablis
Billaud, Jean & André 1 quai de Reugny, 89800 Chablis	**Maladière (Domaine de la)** 14 rue Jules Rathier, 89800 Chablis	
Collet, Jean (& Fils) 1 rue du Panonceau, 89800 Chablis	**Michel, Louis (& Fils)** 11 bd des Ferrières, 89800 Chablis	

Vaucoupin   ♀♀♀♀♀

Commune: Chichée. **Named vineyards:** Vaucopins, Adroit de Vaucopins. **Area under production:** approximately 27 hectares. **Map:** page 137. Although this *climat* is on the right bank it is in the commune of Chichée, the village which lies along the left bank of the Serein. It has a good geological and geographical situation and it is to be regretted that its reputation is not on a level with its fine quality.

Growers	**Bretin, Alain** 9 rue de l'Eglise, 89800 Chablis	**Collon, Guy** 89700 Tonnerre
Bègue, Joël 4 rue Paul Bert, 89800 Chablis	**Carpentier, Bernard** Rue Principale, 89000 Auxerre	**Dauvissat, Lionel** 89800 Fleys
Bocquet, Daniel 89700 Tonnerre	**Carpentier, Fernand** 14 rue de Talmeau, 89800 Chichée	**Degoix, René** 89800 Chichée
Bocquet, Henri 89700 Tonnerre	**Château de Viviers** 89800 Viviers	**Droin, Jean-Paul** 14 bis rue Jean Jaurès, 89800 Chablis

Ellevin, Jean-Pierre 89800 Chichée	**Laroche, Roger** 89800 Fleys	**Molusson Frères (GAEC)** 89800 Chichée
Ermitage des Champs Boisons 89800 Chichée	**Lhoste, Denise (in usufruct)** 36 rue Grande, 89800 Chichée	**Molusson, Patrick** 89800 Chichée
Foulley, Albert (Mme Veuve) 89800 Fleys	**Long Depaquit, Albert (GFA)** 45 rue Auxerroise, 89800 Chablis	**Mothe, Jean-Louis** 89800 Fontenay-près-Chablis
Foulley, Eric Lame/Côte Neuve, 89800 Chichée	**Maurice, Max** 89800 Chichée	**Notton, Jean** 89800 Chichée
Foulley, René 89800 Chichée	**Merschiltz, Alain** 89800 Chichée	**Notton, Monique** Rue de la Paix, 89800 Chichée
Gautheron, Alain 89800 Fleys	**Merschiltz, Lucien** 89800 Chichée	**Pagnier, Roger** Béru, 89700 Tonnerre
Gautheron, Jean 89800 Fleys	**Michaut, Daniel** 89800 Fleys	**Picq, Denis** 89800 Chichée
Grossot, Jean-Pierre 89800 Fleys	**Michaut, Luc** 1 rue de Chablis, 89800 Chichée	**Picq, Jacques** 98800 Chichée
Grossot, Michel 89800 Fleys	**Michaut, Michel** 89800 Chichée	**Pinon, Guy** 89800 Chichée
Jacquinot, Roland 89800 Chichée	**Michaut, René** 89800 Chichée	**Robin, André** 89800 Chichée
Jeanniot, Marius 89800 Chichée	**Michaut, Roger** 89800 Chichée	**Robin, Jean** 89800 Chichée
Laroche, Claude 89800 Chablis	**Molusson, Claude** 89800 Chichée	

Vau de Vey ♟♟♟♟♟

Commune: Beine. **Named vineyards:** La Grande Chaume, Vau de Vey. **Area under production:** approximately 30 hectares. **Map:** page 138. One of the latest arrivals, and the smallest in the family of the *Premiers Crus*. Its standard has yet to assert itself.

Growers

Azo, Hervé
2 rue de Champlain, 89800 Chablis

Bethery, Daniel
4 Moulin du Faubourg, Chablis

Bouvet, Gilbert
Freterive, 73250 St-Pierre d'Albigny

Durup, Jean
Dne de l'Eglantière, 89800 Maligny
Jean Durup has one of the broadest ranges of properties in Chablis, with about 110 hectares of vines. He is greatly attached to his family roots which have gone deep into the land of Maligny over nearly five centuries. He has also undertaken the restoration of Château de Maligny as well as part of the old viticultural estate attached to it. At the end of the nineteenth century, his great grand-father was the last of the workers there, being responsible for the château's vines and cellars. He markets his vast production under the following names: Domaine de l'Eglantière, Château de

The Château de Maligny is in the process of being restored.

Maligny, Domaine de la Paulière and Domaine des Valéry. Jean Durup's personal role in the delimitation of the Chablis appellations has been de-

cisive (though sometimes contentious). As President of the largest viticultural federation of the area, the Fédération des Vignerons du Chablisien, he has

157

seen his efforts crowned with success, despite much controversy. For many years he has been a representative of the Chablis vineyards on the I.N.A.O. Council for Burgundy. In Vau de Vey he cultivates about 14 hectares. Apart from a few vines on Premier Cru land at Chapelots or Montmains, his principal Premier Cru holding is in Maligny, where he owns 17 hectares scattered over the climat of L'Homme Mort, attached to Fourchaume. Jean Durup's professional training accounts for his rigorous management style. He is frequently hailed as one of those who, over the last ten years, have got

Chablis moving again , in an attempt to establish a more comfortable and constant profit margin in place of the violent ups and downs to which it had been prone. Vinification here is carried out in modern installations. A dynamic marketing policy has brought about significant breakthroughs into French and foreign markets.

Malandes (Domaine des)
Rue Auxerroise, 89800 Chablis

Vaux de Vey (SCEA des)
Rue de l'Auxerroise, 89800 Chablis

Vaugiraut   𐎜 𐎜 𐎜 𐎜 𐎜

Commune: Chichée. **Named vineyard:** Vaugiraut. **Area under production:** approximately 3 hectares. **Map:** page 136. Also in the commune of Chichée, but on the left bank, this tiny *climat* can be placed, for quality, in the middle ranks of the *Premiers Crus*. But it is rare for its wines to bear this name.

Growers	Molusson, Patrick 89800 Chichée	Pinon, Guy 89800 Chichée
Merschiltz, Alain 89800 Chichée	Nahan, William 12 rue des Fossés, 89800 Chablis	
Merschiltz, Lucien 89800 Chichée	Notton, Jean 89800 Chichée	

Vau Ligneau   𐎜 𐎜 𐎜 𐎜 𐎜

Commune: Beine. **Named vineyards:** La Forêt, Sur la Forêt, Vau de Longue, Vau Girault, Vau Vigneau. **Area under production:** approximately 17 hectares. **Map:** page 138. One of the very latest arrivals to the club of the *Premiers Crus*, after recent extensions granted by the INAO. This explains why it is presently unknown. But it ought to do well.

Growers	more personal character to his wines. He appears to have succeeded. He sells part of his production in bulk and the rest in bottles, destined mainly for export.	Hamelin, Thierry 89800 Lignorelles
Dauvissat, Jean-Claude (Domaine) La Jouchère, 89800 Beine *Jean-Claude Dauvissat runs an estate of some 23 hectares of good vines. Until recent years he was a member of the Chablis cave coopérative but he withdrew recently, preferring to give a*		Michaut Frères (GAEC) 41 rue du Ruisseau, 89800 Chablis
	Geoffroy, Alain 4 rue de l'Equerre, 89800 Beine	

Vaulorent   𐎜 𐎜 𐎜 𐎜 𐎜

Commune: Fontenay-près-Chablis, Poinchy. **Named vineyards:** La Ferme Couverte, Les Couvertes, Les Quatre Chemins. **Area under production:** approximately 17 hectares. **Map:** page 134. The closest neighbour to Preuses, Vaulorent is a very rare wine, much sought after. Its only handicap is its northern aspect . The *terroir's* potential for making to make good wine is undeniable. In great years it can be sublime, producing even better wine than Fourchaume – but frost is the great energy.

Growers

Auffray (Ancien Domaine)
14 rue Jules Rathier, 89800 Chablis

Bègue, Charles
12 rue de Chitry, 89800 Chablis

Bègue, Joël
4 rue Paul Bert, 89800 Chablis

Dauvissat, Jean
89800 Chablis

De Oliveira, Bernard
89800 Fontenay-près-Chablis

De Oliveira Père & Fils
89800 Fontenay-près-Chablis

Dupas, Henri
89800 Fontenay-près-Chablis

Fèvre frères (GAEC)
89800 Fontenay-près-Chablis

Filippi, Jeanne-Paule (SC)
14 rue Jules Rathier, 89800 Chablis

Gautheron, Félix
89800 Fontenay-près-Chablis

Gautheron, Jean-Michel
89800 Fontenay-près-Chablis

Laroche (SCEA)
67 Grande Rue, 89800 Maligny

Maladière (Domaine de la)
14 rue Jules Rathier, 89800 Chablis

Michel, Louis (& Fils)
11 bd des Ferrières, 89800 Chablis

Mothe, Jean-Louis
89800 Fontenay-près-Chablis

Roy, Raymond & Claude
89800 Fontenay-près-Chablis

Tremblay, Jacques
89800 La Chapelle-Vaupelteigne

Vaupulent ♟ ♟ ♟ ♟ ♟

Communes: Fontenay-près-Chablis, La Chapelle-Vaupelteigne, Poinchy. **Named vineyards:** La Fourchaume, Les Vaupulans, Vau Pulan. **Area under production:** approximately 9 hectares. **Map:** page 134. The most southery of the Fourchaumes *crus* lies opposite Vaulorent, which enables the chardonnay to ripen more. No label bears its name, which is a shame, because its wines could be mistaken for a *Grand Cru*.

Growers

De Oliveira & Lecestre
89800 Fontenay-près-Chablis

Droin Père & Fils (GAEC)
3 rue de Montmain, 89800 Chablis

Duplessis Père & Fils
5 quai de Reugny, 89800 Chablis

Fèvre Frères (GAEC)
89800 Fontenay-près-Chablis

Goulley, Jean
89800 La Chapelle-Vaupelteigne

Malandes (Domaine des)
61 rue Auxerroise, 89800 Chablis

Porcheron, Ulysse
89800 Fontenay-près-Chablis

Vaux Ragons ♟ ♟ ♟ ♟ ♟

Commune: Beine. **Named vineyard:** Vignes des Vaux Ragons. **Area under production:** approximately 13 hectares. **Map:** page 138. An extension of Vau de Vey towards the south, this *climat* has very similar qualities. A young but very promising vineyard.

Growers

Durup, Jean
Dne de l'Eglantière, 89800 Chablis

Laroche (SCEA)
67 Grande Rue, 89800 Maligny

Vosgros ♙♙♙♙♙

Commune: Chichée. **Named vineyards:** Vosgros, Adroit de Vosgros. **Area under production:** approximately 7 hectares. **Map:** page 136. A "historic" *Premier Cru*, like its neighbour Vaugiraut, in the vineyards of Chichée. It can be a good buy, for without being a great star, this *climat* offers robust, sinewy and well-balanced wines.

Growers

Droin, Jean-Paul
14 bis rue Jean Jaurès, 89800 Chablis

Ellevin, Jean-Pierre
89800 Chichée

Ermitage des Champs Boisons
89800 Chichée

Guette Soleil
89800 Chablis

Lavaud, Bernard
89800 Chablis

Maurice, Max
89800 Chichée

Molusson, Claude
89800 Chichée

Notton, Monique
Rue de la Paix, 89800 Chichée

Picq, Gilbert & Fils
89800 Chichée

Race, Christian
89800 Chablis

Race, Jacques
89800 Chablis

Robin, Jean
89800 Chichée

Caught by the sun, the vines' support-wires dazzle the eye.

Chablis and Petit-Chablis

A typical Chablis landscape. In the distance, the village of Viviers.

The following catalogue lists the communes making up the Chablis region. Mention is made under each heading of all the principal growers registering annual harvest return figures in the Chablis or Petit-Chablis AOCs. The surface areas of the vineyards of each commune are given as a general indication. They contain non-AOC vineyards (producing "grand ordinaire" or ordinary white Burgundy, table wine, etc.). The difference in quality between these two appellations should be stressed. Petit-Chablis has no claims other than that of being a likeable "ready-to-drink" wine, whereas the appellation Chablis can often signify very respectable bottles.

Beine

Total area of vines under production	Quantity declared as AOC in 1987		
	Chablis 1er Cru	Chablis	Petit-Chablis
149.71 ha	2 000 hl	6 297 hl	537 hl

Alphabetically the first commune in the Chablis region. It is also the first that you encounter as you leave the Autoroute du Soleil (at the South Auxerre junction). Four miles to the east of the village of Chablis it has demonstrated its modern outlook with the construction of an artificial lake, covering some 15 hectares, for sprinkling the vines against frost. The vineyards of Beine were recently extended as a result of the latest delimitation of the appellations. Not only the "historic" *Premier Cru* of Trœsmes, but also its peers, Vau Ligneau and Vau de Vey are to be found here. Out of a population of some 350 inhabitants, about forty people register harvest figures (1984), of whom nine belong to the *cave coopérative*, La Chablisienne. The valleys upstream of the lake afford picturesque walks. The village, half in the present, half in the past, provides an unruffled picture of life in the Chablis region. In the tenth century the land of *Beina* was dependent on the *seigneurie* of Maligny, and this little village used to be encircled by protective ramparts. Its church was founded in the thirteenth century, but every succeeding century has left its mark.

In 1987, the production of the commune of Beine was approximately 2,000 hectolitres of *Premier Cru* Chablis, 6,300 hectolitres of Chablis and 540 hectolitres of Petit-Chablis. These figures are likely to increase with new plantings. One interesting point: the Chambre d'Agriculture is also a proprietor here. For hungry visitors, the *Relais de Chablis* in Beine is a pleasant and relatively simple stopping-off point.

Growers

Bellot, Louis
45 Grande Rue   86 42 41 66

Blanvillain, Jacques
9 rue du Ruisseau   86 42 40 63

Chambre d'Agriculture

Dauvissat, Jean-Claude
2 Grande Rue   86 42 42 66

Dauvissat, Jean-Claude (Domaine)
La Jouchère   86 42 42 65

Franclet, Robert
7 Grande Rue   86 42 42 84

Geoffroy, Alain
4 rue de l'Equerre   86 42 43 76

Hugot, Jean

Lefort, Rémy
2 du Grand Four   86 42 43 75

Michaut Frères (GAEC)
41 rue du Ruisseau   86 42 43 71

Mosnier, Sylvain
4 rue Derrière les Murs   86 42 43 96

Naulin, Jean-Marie
6 rue du Carouge

Naulin, Robert
6 rue du Carouge   86 42 40 47

Patrice, André
5 ruelle du Grand Four   86 42 42 07

Patrice, Gérard
5 rue des Fossés   86 42 43 10

Roblot, Daniel
Rue Porte d'Auxerre   86 42 43 00

Villain, Robert
8 chemin des Fossés   86 42 42 94

Zozime, Roger
56 Grande Rue   86 42 43 12

Béru

Total area of vines under production	Quantity declared as AOC in 1987		
	Chablis 1er Cru	Chablis	Petit-Chablis
29.98 ha	111 hl	1 618 hl	17 hl

"The shortest road is the quickest" is the splendid motto of the Le Court de Béru family, still proprietors today of the château whose earliest foundations go back to the seventeenth century. Béru, once a fortified village, has had a chequered history. Invasion, pillage and fire followed one after the other. Its site dominates the valley of the Serein and the panoramas it offers are among the most spectacular in the region. According to Robert Fèvre, a historian of the area, the inhabitants of Béru were formerly called *Les Cacousas*, a nickname which came from the large nut called *cacou* in local dialect. There was a time when Béru was the principal source of these nuts.

With twenty growers registering harvest return figures (of whom three belong to the *coopérative*), Béru is one of the most modest of Chablis communes in viticultural terms. Its main production is of simple AOC Chablis. But it has an undeniably long history, for it formed part of the estates of the abbey of Pontigny in the twelfth and thirteenth centuries. Afterwards, the area round Béru belonged to the Miles de Noyers family, which was perhaps the real origin of the *Cacousas* (*noyer* in French meaning walnut tree.)

The little church of Sainte-Madeleine merits a short visit. Its origins go back to the very beginning of the eighteenth century, and until the Revolution its high-pitched bell chimed the hours for the vignerons. It was christened "La Couine" ("The Squeak").

Growers	
Bègue, Bernard	
Bègue, Daniel	86 75 93 05
Bègue, Denis	86 75 90 58
Bègue, Jacques	86 75 92 28
Bocquet, Daniel	86 75 92 25
Bocquet, Henri	86 75 90 82
Pagnier, Roger	86 75 90 69
Soupé, Edouard	86 75 90 63

The Château of Béru

Chablis

Total area of vines under production	Quantity declared as AOC in 1987			
	Chablis Grand Cru	Chablis 1er Cru	Chablis	Petit-Chablis
788.89 ha	4 425 hl	19 015 hl	20 790 hl	1 389 hl

Various explanations exist as to the origin of the name. The most likely one traces *Chablis* back to the Latin word *caplum*, or cable, from the cable that used to be stretched across the Serein to help ford it in Roman times. It is said that the Emperor Probus had the first vines planted here at the end of the third century. In the Middle Ages, Chablis was a large village protected by ramparts flanked with thirty or so watchtowers and surrounded by a forty-foot wide moat. Four principal postern-gates controlled access to the village. Today only one remains, called the Chenneton Gate. The lower part of the village contains houses constructed between the fourteenth and the eighteenth centuries, one of the finest being the Obédiencerie, which houses a thirteenth-century press. Curiously, Chablis has a "rue des Juifs" ("Jews' Road") in which there is a house in Renaissance style called the Synagogue. No one knows its origins.

The neighbouring villages of Fyé, Milly and Poinchy amalgamated with the commune of Chablis a few years ago. Today, there are about 2,500 inhabitants. Slightly over 350 growers register harvest return figures, of whom about twelve belong to the *coopérative*. Almost all the *Grands Crus* and several *Premiers Crus*, including the most famous names, lie within this commune.

Growers

Auffray (Ancien Domaine)
14 rue Jules Rathier

Baillard (SCEA du Domaine)
20 avenue d'Oberwesel

Bègue, Jean
11 rue Jules Rathier   86 42 15 00

Bègue, Joël
4 rue Paul Bert   86 42 16 65

Bègue, Maurice
6 rue Abel Hovelacque   86 42 16 45

Besson, Alain
19 rue Emile Zola   86 42 19 53

Besson, Félix
28 rue de Reugny   86 42 11 00

Billaud-Simon & Fils
Quai de Reugny   86 42 10 33

Bouchard, Pascal
17 boulevard Lamarque   86 42 18 64

Collet, Claude
10 rue Abel Hovelacque   86 42 10 65

Collet, Jean & Fils
1 rue du Panonceau   86 42 11 93

Dauvissat, René & Vincent
8 rue Emile Zola   86 42 11 58

Defaix, Bernard
17 rue du Château   86 42 40 75

Droin, Jean-Paul
14 bis rue Jean Jaurès   86 42 16 78

Duplessis, Marcel & Gérard
5 quai de Reugny   86 42 10 35

Faffay, Thierry

Feuillebois, Jean
13 rue de Reugny   86 42 14 07

Feuillebois, Jean-Claude
18 bd Tacussel   86 42 12 89

Feuillebois, René
6 rue de Montmain   86 42 17 69

Fèvre, Maurice
17 av. Aristide-Briand   86 42 11 21

Fèvre, René
28 rue de Chichée   86 42 18 68

The Obédiencerie once belonged to the abbey of St-Martin de Tours.

Fèvre, William
14 rue Jules Rathier   86 42 12 51

Filippi, Jeanne-Paule (SC)
14 rue Jules Rathier

Gautherin, Raoul
6 bd Lamarque   86 42 11 86

Gouailhardou, Jean-Pierre
18 rue Auxerroise   86 42 18 81

Grumet, André
25 rue Abel Hovelacque   86 42 14 64

Laroche, Henri
10 rue Auxerroise   86 42 14 30

Jacquin, Jean
30 bis rue de Chichée   86 42 16 32

Lavens, Jules
13 bis rue Jules Rathier   86 42 14 59

Lavens, Michel
45 HLM Les Picards

Long Depaquit, A. (Domaine)
45 rue Auxerroise   86 42 11 13

| Malandes (Domaine des) | |
| Rue Auxerroise | 86 42 41 37 |

| Michel, Louis (& Fils) | |
| 11 bd Ferrières | 86 42 10 24 |

| Michel, Maurice | |
| 9 rue Emile Zola | 86 42 14 37 |

| Mignard, Christian | |
| 40 rue Auxerroise | 86 42 12 27 |

| Moreau, Roger | |
| 5 rue des Fossés | 86 42 14 83 |

| Moreau, J. (& Fils) | |
| Route d'Auxerre | 86 42 40 70 |

| Pinson, Louis (Domaine) | |
| 5 quai Voltaire | 86 42 10 26 |

| Race, Denis | |
| 16 rue de Chichée | 86 42 45 87 |

Chablis: the old walls.

| Race, Suzanne | |
| 14 rue de Chichée | |

| Robin, Alain | |
| 24 bis rue Jean Jaurès | 86 42 18 72 |

| Robin, Jean-Pierre | |
| 13 rue Berthelot | |

| Robin, Madeleine | |
| 2 rue des Juifs | 86 42 44 87 |

| Robin, Michel | |
| 2 rue du Puits | 86 42 17 40 |

| Rogié, André | |
| Chemin des Petits Dieux | 86 42 12 20 |

| Rogié, François | |
| Clos des Dieux | |

| Servin, Bernard | |
| 3 av. Jean Jaurès | 86 42 12 67 |

| Servin, Marcel | |
| 20 av. d'Oberwesel | 86 42 12 94 |

| Simon, Christian | |
| 24 avenue Jean Jaurès | |

| Simonnet Fèbvre & Fils | |
| 9 av. Oberwesel | 86 42 11 73 |

| Soupé, Jean-Claude | |
| 32 av. Oberwesel | 86 42 18 27 |

| Testut Frères (SCEA) | |
| 38 rue des Moulins | 86 42 45 00 |

| Tremblay, Gérard | |
| 12 rue de Poinchy | 86 42 40 98 |

| Tremblay, Louis | |
| 1 rue des Moulins | 86 42 11 08 |

| Vauroux (Domaine de) | 86 42 10 37 |

| Vocoret & Fils | |
| 16 rue Emile Zola | 86 42 12 53 |

Chemilly-sur-Serein

Total area of vines under production	Quantity declared as AOC in 1987		
	Chablis 1er Cru	Chablis	Petit-Chablis
90.67 ha	111 hl	4 793 hl	507 hl

The name *Chemelliacum* can be traced back to the beginning of the twelfth century. On the boundary between Burgundy and Champagne, Chemilly-sur-Serein, like Béru, for many years belonged to the Count de Noyers. It was owned by the Budé family during the lifetime of Guillaume Budé, the famous philologist , humanist, and friend of Erasmus and Rabelais, in the fifteenth century. In the eighteenth century the village was twice completely destroyed by fire. The château was reconstructed two hundred years later by the Baron de Varange.

The terrain of Chemilly-sur-Serein has no *Premiers Crus*, but a number of its growers also have vines in Fourchaume and Vosgros. In Chablis, it is unusual to own parcels in two or three different communes. As elsewhere, several growers produce small quantities of Bourgogne Aligoté or Passe Tout Grains for the consumption of family and friends. There is also considerable production of AOC Chablis, approaching 4,500 hectolitres yearly, of which nearly a third is registered by the firm of Guette-Soleil-Vilain. Out of a population of 170 inhabitants there are some forty or so growers, sixteen of whom belong to the *cave coopérative*, La Chablisienne.

Growers	Kaczmar, Edmond		Racé, Christian	86 42 12 85
	Rue du Pont	86 42 13 37		
			Racé, Jacques	86 42 12 39
Detolle, Georges 86 42 13 39	Lavaud, Bernard	86 42 12 60		
			Vilain, Clovis	86 42 11 67
Detolle, Henri (Mme Veuve)	Lavaud, Thierry			
			Vilain, Gabriel	
Detolle, Maurice	Lompré, Daniel	86 42 19 28		
			Vilain, Henri	86 42 18 08
Guette-Soleil-Vilain (GAEC)	Martin, Paul	86 42 15 87		

Chichée

Total area of vines under production	Quantity declared as AOC in 1987		
	Chablis 1er Cru	Chablis	Petit-Chablis
121.22 ha	1 211 hl	5 461 hl	46 hl

This charming village to the south-east of Chablis, lies on the left bank of the Serein. It has preserved its mediaeval layout, with narrow alleys running off the main street. Its fifteenth-century church deserves classification as a historic monument. Formerly, flocks grazed along the river, on pastures which are now the preserve of *boules* players. Chichée has maintained an agricultural character typical of lower Burgundy, and its people have a reputation for toughness. Local tradition has it that in the 1860s, three very ambitious brothers competed with one another to become the most prosperous man in the village. One of them used to throw his loaf of bread as far as he could into the vines, after eating a mouthful or two. "The harder it is, the happier I am!" he would say, rubbing his hands.

The land covered by the commune, which covers 1,800 hectares, stretches out on either side of the Serein. Here we find the excellent *crus* of Vaucoupin, Vosgiraud and Vosgros. Chichée numbers at least sixty growers registering their harvest, among whom six belong to the *coopérative*.

The village of Chichée among its woods and vines.

Growers

Carpentier, Fernand
14 rue de Talmeau   86 42 12 32

Degoix, René   86 42 13 45

Ellevin, Jean-Pierre   86 42 44 24

Gasser, Jean
1 place de la Gare   86 42 19 11

Jacquinot, Roland
4 rue Neuve du Prieuré 86 42 13 62

Maurice, Max
Rue de Chablis   86 42 15 75

Merschiltz, Alain
8 chemin de l'Araignée 86 42 46 14

Merschiltz, Lucien
43 Grande Rue   86 42 11 99

Michaut, Luc
1 rue de Chablis   86 42 11 76

Michaut, Michel   86 42 18 25

Michaut René	86 42 18 51	Picq, Denis	86 42 18 74	Robin, André (Mme Veuve)	
				44 Grande Rue	86 42 19 55
Michaut, Roger		Picq, Gilbert & Fils (GAEC)			
			86 42 18 30	Robin, Jean	
Molusson Frères (GAEC)				Grande Rue	86 42 17 31
46 Grande Rue	86 42 12 95	Picq, Jacques	86 42 15 51		
				Sallé, Louis	
Notton, Jean		Pinon, Guy	86 42 18 57	Ermitage des Champs Boisons	
Impasse Saint-Paul	86 42 10 04				86 42 12 56

Courgis

Total area of vines under production	Quantity declared as AOC in 1987		
	Chablis 1er Cru	Chablis	Petit-Chablis
120.47 ha	1 422 hl	4 955 hl	141 hl

The writer Restif de La Bretonne, who came from Sacy, lived in Courgis, where his brother Edme was priest, for nearly three years. In his work *La vie de mon père* he mentions this village frequently. Since 1555, the church has housed a thorn from the Crown of Thorns, preserved in a superb reliquary, and said to have been brought back to France by Godefroy de Bouillon's crusaders in about the year 1100. The crystal and silver-gilt reliquary dates from the seventeenth century, and was probably commissioned by the clergy when the lord of the area, Jacques Ferrand, Baron of Courgis, donated the thorn to the parish in 1630.

Courgis is to the south-west of Chablis, close to the Autoroute du Soleil (but there is no direct exit off to the village). Standing on its hillside, the little village is very picturesque. The vineyards of Courgis contain the *Premiers Crus* of Côte de Cuissy, Les Beauregards, Les Landes et Verjuts and Chaume de Talvat. There are nearly ninety growers registering harvest figures, of whom thirty five belong to La Chablisienne. From the D62 road, which crosses Courgis on the way to Chablis, the walker has a splendid view over the valley of the Serein.

Growers

Adine, Christian		**Dufour, Robert**	
Rue R. de La Bretonne	86 41 40 28	Rue Jacques Ferrand	86 41 41 82

Adine, Madeleine
Rue Nicolas Froin

Adine, Maurice
Rue R. de La Bretonne 86 41 42 98

Barbier, Pierre (Mme Veuve)
Rue Jeannette Rousseau

Bouc, Gabriel
Route de Préhy 86 41 43 51

Bouc, Jacques
Grande Rue 86 41 40 57

Cathelin, Bernard 86 41 40 66

Chapotin, Philibert 86 41 41 12

Dufour, Jean-Robert
Rue Jacques Ferrand

Dufour, Robert
Rue Jacques Ferrand 86 41 41 82

Dupré, André
Rue Jeannette Rousseau 86 41 42 10

Dupré, Gilbert

Foulley, Jacques

Foulley, Philippe
Rue Jacques Ferrand 86 41 43 57

George, Michel
Rue du Four Banal 86 41 40 06

Landais, Roger
Grande Rue 86 41 42 53

Maingonnat, Raymond (Mme Veuve)
86 41 42 06

Martin, Jean-Claude
Rue Larminat 86 41 40 33

Picq, Georges
Gde Rue N. Droin 86 41 43 14

Quittot, Gilbert 86 41 40 41

Race, André
Rue du Four Banal 86 41 44 72

Race, Bernard
Rue Jacques Ferrand 86 41 42 76

Race, Gilbert
Rue des Pressoirs 86 41 41 09

Race, Rémy
Grande Rue 86 41 41 97

Rétif, Pierre
Rue Jacques Ferrand 86 41 41 73

Fleys

Total area of vines under production	Quantity declared as AOC in 1987		
	Chablis 1er Cru	Chablis	Petit-Chablis
84.6 ha	2 059 hl	2 765 hl	51 hl

Fleys can be justifiably proud possessing one of the best *Premiers Crus* in the Chablis region, Mont de Milieu, as well as the good *climats* of Morein, Côte des Prés Girots and Les Fourneaux. The viticultural *terrain* of this commune covers some 80 hectares out of a total area of nearly 800 hectares. This is the famous Kimmeridgian *terroir* cultivated by Lionel Dauvissat, Robert Rousseau and Laroche Père & Fils, all excellent growers.

According to the historian Robert Fèvre, the inhabitants of Fleys were formerly called *Gougueys*, from the dialect word for a snail. It does not surprise me that there were once huge quantities of snails here, for Fleys is also called the "land of springs". The most famous is that of La Coudre, which is said to have been divined by a hazel-branch (*coudrier* in French). Fleys' Latin name, *Flaiacum*, is a reference to the abundance of running water, which has encouraged people to settle here since earthest times. Up to the nineteenth century fields of hemp were cultivated, particularly in the hamlet of La Fonte, surrounded by pools in which the hemp was soaked. Traces of a Roman road demonstrate the age of the site of Fleys. The church of Saint-Nicolas, which has been undergoing restoration for the last twenty years, is a fine example of regional architecture of the Renaissance period.

Growers

	Gautheron, Jean	86 42 15 19	Michaut, André Rue Fontaine 86 42 11 84
	Grossot, Jean-Pierre	86 42 44 64	Michaut, Daniel
Aufrere, Dominique 86 42 10 15	Grossot, Michel	86 42 14 89	Rue Fontaine 86 42 11 84
Couperot, Alain 86 42 14 69	Laroche, Claude	86 42 13 56	Nicolle, Paul 86 42 15 09
Dauvissat, Lionel 86 42 18 42	Laroche, Roger Route Nationale	86 42 10 57	Nicolle, Robert 86 42 19 30
Foulley, Albert (Mme Veuve) 86 42 13 33	Lécullier, René (Mme Veuve)		Philippon, André 86 42 13 73
Fournillon, Bernard 86 42 15 44	Lesage, Paulette		Rousseau, Robert Route de Chapelle 86 42 15 93
Gautheron, Alain 86 42 44 34	Lesage, René (Mme Veuve) 86 42 12 80		

Fontenay-près-Chablis

Total area of vines under production	Quantity declared as AOC in 1987		
	Chablis 1er Cru	Chablis	Petit-Chablis
136.42 ha	2 049 hl	4 123 hl	1 320 hl

On May 11, 1745, the battle of Fontenoy did not take place at Fontenay-près-Chablis, however much certain local historians wish that it had. Nor was it the scene of the battle of Fontanetum in which Charles the Bald, Lothaire and Louis le Germanique fought nine centuries earlier. On the other hand, on June 18, 1818, a house in the heart of the village was completely destroyed by water which cascaded down the hillside, forming waves twelve feet high. A commemorative stone relates that it was "reconstructed by the munificence of LL. AA. RR. Madame la Duchesse d'Angoulême and Monsieur le Duc de Berry. O noble blood of the Bourbons, ye virtuous Princes, long may you live! Reign for ever over France. May love and gratitude be ever your due! The reign of the Bourbons is a gift of Heaven."

The land of Fontenay is a gift of the gods, whose beneficence extends over the Côte de Fontenay and part of the *climats* of Vaulorent and Vaupulent. The little commune of Fontenay, which numbers 180 inhabitants in an area of 540 hectares, registers harvest return figures from barely sixty growers, of whom twenty belong to the *coopérative*. It is situated in the north-eastern part of the "golden semicircle" which has Chablis as its centre, on the right bank of the Serein, from La Chapelle-Vaupelteigne to Chichée.

Growers	De Oliveira Père & Fils (GAEC)	Porcheron, Ulysse
	Dupas, Henri 86 42 11 41	Rousseau, Jean-Pierre
Bérilley, Rolande 86 42 13 72	Dupas, Michèle	Rousseau, Pierre
Carré Frères (Pierre & Robert)		Rue Principale 86 42 11 40
86 42 44 15	Fèvre Frères (GAEC) 86 42 11 48	Roy, Raymond & Claude 86 42 10 36
Colombier (GAEC du)	Habert, Richard 86 42 11 71	Vrignaud, Michel 86 42 15 69
De Oliveira, Bernard 86 42 14 65	Lecestre, André 86 42 11 59	
De Oliveira Lecestre (GAEC)	Lourdou, René 86 42 15 11	

Fyé

Total area of vines under production	Quantity declared as AOC in 1987		
	Chablis 1er Cru	Chablis	Petit-Chablis
34 ha	302 hl	985 hl	404 hl

This little parish at the top of the valley of Bréchain is today absorbed into the commune of Chablis. The vineyards of Fyé are the most consistent in quality in Chablis. Apart from its *Grands Crus*, it can also claim the famous Montée de Tonnerre, part of Mont de Milieu and the *cru* of Côte de Bréchain, which is distinguished by its finesse. For myself, I confess a soft spot for the *climats* of Chapelot and Pied d'Aloue.

Growers	Fèvre, Régis Chemin Ferme 86 42 13 26	
	Ratel, Annick	
Bonnet, Jean-Marie	Renaud, André	
Bonnet, Marcel 86 42 13 69	Renaud, Robert	
Bonnet, Maurice (Mme Veuve)		
Dauvissat, Michel 7 rue Fyé 86 42 12 86		

Fyé from the Côte de Bréchain.

La Chapelle-Vaupelteigne

Total area of vines under production	Quantity declared as AOC in 1987		
	Chablis 1er Cru	Chablis	Petit-Chablis
122.32 ha	2 013 hl	4 843 hl	326 hl

This commune stretches out along the valley of the Serein downstream from Chablis. It covers only 504 hectares and there are scarcely 140 inhabitants, but its 120 hectares of vineyards are of remarkable quality. To give honour where it is due, the illustrious Fourchaume reigns here. Its name, and that of L'Homme Mort, which extends northwards from it, have a long history. In 1970 Jean Duchâtel, the priest of Chablis, began an archaeological excavation which brought to light traces of a Roman settlement. Formerly there were flour-mills along the Serein, and probably tanneries where animal skins were dressed, and from which came the name of Vaupelteigne (pelts). The chapel itself, dedicated to Our Lady and Saint Didier, was founded in the year 903.

La Chapelle-Vaupelteigne as a commune produces the highest ratio of *Premier Cru* Chablis to the extent of land under vines. This translates into real terms the excellent nature of the *terroir*. Seventeen people belong to the *cave coopérative* and there are forty independent growers. The wines of La Chapelle-Vaupelteigne have always been sought after by good wine merchants and dedicated wine-lovers.

Growers		Defert, René		Thouveray, Patrick	
Chantemerle (GAEC de)		Foynat, Pierre	86 42 41 33	Tremblay, Annette Rue Principale	86 42 41 10
Chenevières (GAEC des)		Goulley, Jean Vallée des Rosiers	86 42 40 85	Tremblay, Gabrielle	86 42 43 32
Crochot, Alain	86 42 42 82	La Fourchaume (GAEC)		Tremblay, Henri	86 42 43 68
Crochot, Armand	86 42 40 23	Lhoste, Maurice	86 42 43 04	Tremblay, Jacques	86 42 40 03
Dauvissat Père & Fils	86 42 43 39	Rutem, Maurice	86 42 42 86	Tupinier, Marcel	86 42 42 29

Lignorelles

Total area of vines under production	Quantity declared as AOC in 1987		
	Chablis 1er Cru	Chablis	Petit-Chablis
184.83 ha	619 hl	6 532 hl	3 246 hl

At the time of the delimitation of the Chablis vignoble, it was decided that that part of the "Petit-Chablis" appellation situated on "heavy soil" should lose its right to this appellation as from January 1, 2000. At the present time, following the reorganization of a section of the territory, some of the vineyards of Lignorelles are in the process of being transferred and will find a new home in the area of the "Chablis" appellation.

On the north-western boundaries of the Chablis region, Lignorelles has no *Premiers Crus*, but five of its growers register this appellation from vines they own in one or other of the neighbouring communes. Lignorelles holds up well as a Chablis AOC and, as at

Maligny and Beine, its production in Petit-Chablis will be on the increase. Ten growers belong to La Chablisienne and there are fifty or so people registering harvest returns.

Growers

Beaufumé, Jean	86 47 44 46				
Crochot, Henri Route d'Auxerre	86 47 40 06				
Fassier, Christiane	86 47 48 62				
Gallois, Christiane					
Gallois, Marcellin	86 47 41 18				
Gallois, Vincent Jean-Paul					
Hamelin, Marc	86 47 41 80				
Hamelin, Thierry	86 47 52 79				
Lacour, Thierry	86 47 52 34	Massé, Georges	86 47 41 49	Rey, René	86 47 43 03
Lavantureux, Gilberte		Pautré, Francis		Ronsien (SCEA de)	
Lavantureux, Luc	86 47 44 56	Pautré Père & Fils	86 47 42 32	Tremblay, Suzanne	
Lavantureux, Roland		Petit, Jean-Paul		Vandewiele, Elisabeth	
L'Orme à Véron (SCA de)	86 47 41 60	Pourantru, Noël Rte de Ligny-le-Châtel	86 47 48 88	Vandewiele, Gérard	86 47 41 87
Massé, Didier		Rey, Jean-Marie			

The church of Lignorelles stands guard over the vineyards.

Ligny-le-Châtel

Total area of vines under production	Quantity declared as AOC in 1987		
	Chablis 1er Cru	Chablis	Petit-Chablis
4.13 ha	181 hl	55 hl	10 hl

This commune, the most northerly of the Chablis region, is also the largest after Chablis, with more than one thousand inhabitants. Formerly, the village was divided into two parishes: Ligny-la-Ville and Ligny-le-Château, governed successively by the Colberts and the Montmorencys. In the thirteenth century, Marguerite de Bourgogne founded a leper hospital here. The origins of the village are very ancient: numerous Merovingian and Carolingian tombs have been discovered. One branch of the Serein flows through the village and whitebait are fished from it to accompany the excellent Petit-Chablis of this area. Not far away is the abbey of Pontigny which, as mentioned before, had such influence over the southern vineyards. The production of Ligny-le-Châtel is on a small scale, involving only forty growers who produce mainly for domestic consumption. Several slopes within the "Chablis" appellation are to be planted with new vineyards in the near future.

Grower

	Fromont, Jean 8 rue Guy Dupas 86 47 43 81

Maligny

Total area of vines under production	Quantity declared as AOC in 1987		
	Chablis 1er Cru	Chablis	Petit-Chablis
168.60 ha	2 479 hl	6 555 hl	814 hl

After Chablis, this is undoubtedly the liveliest of the communes of the Chablis region and also the most dynamic in its viticulture. The growers of Maligny have always been opposed to Chablis "conservatism" and have played a large part in developing the vineyards. Maligny is at the tip of the Kimmeridgian *terroir* in the old meaning of the word, but its Chablis appellation vineyards are mainly on Portland limestone. The southern part contains the *Premier Cru* L'Homme Mort, more or less absorbed into Fourchaume. The rest is AOC Chablis and Petit-Chablis.

Since the reorganization of this commune, plantings of AOC Chablis seem to be on the increase. The growers of Maligny protect their interests most vigorously, following the example of Jean Durup, president of the Fédération des Vignerons du Chablisien, the principal viticultural federation of the Chablis appellation.

The Portland soil is certainly very promising land for the development of vineyards producing Chablis wines that can keep one step ahead of California chardonnay!

About seventy growers register their harvest returns in Maligny, of whom eight belong to the *coopérative* , and a dozen produce *Premier Cru* wines.

Growers			
	Jolly, Paul (Mme Veuve) 4 rue Auxerroise 86 47 40 75	Lorot, Max 2 bis rue des Plantes 86 47 45 76	
Baillard, Henri 6 rue du Temple 86 47 48 07	Jolly, Roberte 2 rue Auxerroise 86 47 42 31	Séguinot, Daniel 2 rue de Méré 86 47 51 40	
Courtault, Jean-Claude 4 rue du Moulin 86 47 44 76	Jossot, Blanche 49 Grande Rue 86 47 46 32	Séguinot, Roger 4 rue de Méré 86 47 44 42	
Di-Blas, Robert 8A rue de Bourgogne 86 47 43 30	Jossot, Paul 49 Grande Rue	Vocoret, Maurice Rue de Beaune 86 47 40 86	
Durup, Jean Domaine de l'Eglantière 86 47 44 49	Laroche, Paul Chemin des Hâtes 86 47 49 16	Vocoret, Yvon Rue de Beaune 86 47 51 60	
Floc'h, Jean-Pierre 3 rue des Ecoles 86 47 52 42	Lasnier, Pierre 19 rue de Chanteprime 86 47 44 01		

Milly

Total area of vines under production	Quantity declared as AOC in 1987		
	Chablis 1er Cru	Chablis	Petit-Chablis
76 ha	1 745 hl	2 040 hl	40 hl

Today Milly is virtually the western entrance to the village of Chablis. The name takes its origins from the Miles de Noyers family, which for several centuries ruled over Milly and presided over the famous vineyards of Les Lys and Côte de Léchet and their noble wines.

Since its amalgamation with Chablis, Milly no longer has, administratively speaking, a separate identity but its inhabitants are keen to preserve the "difference". If you ask them where they come from, they will reply with pride "from Milly".

Growers		Bourcey, Roland	86 42 43 49	Fourrey, Robert	
Azo, Hervé	86 42 43 56	Coulaudin, Henri	86 42 42 01	Jannet, Jean	86 42 13 01
Barat, Bernard		Defaix, Etienne	86 42 42 05	Peigne, Fernand	
Barat, Michel		Defaix, Jean 17 rue de Champlain	86 42 43 27	Prain, Frédéric	86 42 40 82
Bourcey, Jean	86 42 43 67	Fourrey, Jean-Jack	86 42 44 04	Villetard, Pierre	86 42 42 19

Poilly-sur-Serein

Total area of vines under production	Quantity declared as AOC in 1987		
	Chablis 1er Cru	Chablis	Petit-Chablis
10.70 ha	nil	641 hl	nil

Poilly-sur-Serein occupies the south-eastern tip of the Chablis region. According to Michel de la Torre, from whom I have already borrowed a few historical facts, from his *Guide de l'Art et de la Nature,* for the *département* of the Yonne (Ed. Berger-Levraut, 1981), Poilly-sur-Serein was part of the feudal lands of the seigniory of Tonnerre, to which the Miles de Noyers, Budés, La Trémoilles, etc., succeeded. When the railway was constructed, traces of a Gallo-Roman villa were discovered.

If each village of the area had its own particular industry (leather, timber, hemp, chalk), Poilly-sur-Serein has always specialized in pottery, exploiting a vein of clayey marl (known as "the bad lands") which runs along the Serein, finishing in a point on the edge of the village. Today, Madame Esther Tjebbes carries on the tradition and welcomes visitors in high season.

The wine production of Poilly-sur-Serein is extremely modest, with just five producers of AOC Chablis. Almost all the harvest goes to the *cave coopérative*, La Chablisienne.

Growers

Malaquin, Claude
Rue Lacey   86 75 90 47

Moreau, Jacques   86 75 90 23

Moreau, Pascal
Ferme Liberté   86 75 92 54

Poilly-sur-Serein, a discreet little village.

Poinchy

Total area of vines under production	Quantity declared as AOC in 1987		
	Chablis 1er Cru	Chablis	Petit-Chablis
26.33 ha	452 hl	683 hl	16 hl

This charming and delightfully picturesque village had barely ninety inhabitants when it was absorbed into Chablis. Its vineyards are remarkable for containing the *Premiers Crus* Vaulorent and Beauroy.

Madame Magarian, regional poet and author of the tales and legends *Les quatre fils du toron*, had vineyards at Poinchy.

The mill at Poinchy: dignified country splendour.

Growers

Chatelain, André (Mme Veuve)

Chatelain, Claude
39 rue du Château   86 42 41 70

Coquard, Madeleine

Duchemin, Michel

Guitton, Patrice

Jannet, Jacqueline
Rue Trœme   86 42 40 61

Simonot, Louis
27 rue de Poinchy   86 42 42 38

Simonot, Rémy
Rue Trœme   86 42 40 27

Soleil (GAEC)

Préhy

Total area of vines under production	Quantity declared as AOC in 1987		
	Chablis 1er Cru	Chablis	Petit-Chablis
68.47 ha	162 hl	3 736 hl	163 hl

This commune has amalgamated with Saint-Cyr-les-Colons, which has thus become linked to the Chablis region.

Its inhabitants have in the past upheld that staunchest of Burgundian virtues, fortitude in the face of adversity, but they can only be pushed so far before springing to the defence of their territory. I can recall no better illustration of this than the following extracts from the story "The Prussians in Préhy in December 1870", by A.M. Lodève, which appeared in the *Echo d'Auxerre* in May-June 1973, and I cannot resist quoting here. "When the town of Auxerre had just surrendered, a platoon of Prussians took up position in Saint-Cyr-les-Colons. From there, six or so men went to be quartered in the neighbouring village

174

of Préhy, where the inhabitants lodged them after a fashion. For their first meal in Préhy, the Prussian installed themselves in old mother Turpin's inn where there was always good food to be had and the portions were copious. That at any rate is what was said by the carters who used to transport goods from Vermenton to Chablis. She had laid up abundant provisions right from the beginning of the war and, in addition, she kept chickens, rabbits and a pig, helped by her maid Louison. The Prussians installed themselves noisily at one of the tables in the café and, to the great surprise of the innkeeper, speaking in pidgin French with a heavy German accent, ordered a meal which would have fed a large part of the village, namely: six omelettes each made with six eggs, boiled cabbage with two dozen sausages and six pounds of salt pork, rabbit stew in Irancy wine, three roast chickens, a leg of mutton with haricot beans, two pounds of cheese, all this to be accompanied by a huge bowl of potatoes which served as bread and washed down with an old bottle of local eau-de-vie. However, because of wartime restrictions, the leg of mutton had to be replaced by a huge *terrine de pâté de campagne.*

"When the six omelettes, slightly runny, were brought to table, the chief of the Prussians turned to Madame Turpin and said *Gut* (pronounced *goot*, stressing the t), which in German means good. But old mother Turpin knew no modern language other than the Morvan dialect; she thought that the enemy, being suspicious, was asking her to taste (in French, *goûte* means taste) all the dishes to be certain that they contained no poison. And the stout-hearted woman tasted the six omelettes, the cabbage, the stew, the three chickens, the cheese and even the brandy, even though she had already had her evening meal... The chief of the Prussians believing this to be a local custom guffawed uproariously. The Prussians then drank a second, then a third bottle of eau-de-vie and began to bawl out songs of their homeland, so much so that poor old Louison fled into tears and shut herself in her bedroom.

"The Prussian who was lodging with old Monsieur Isidore on the Vaucharmes road, was fairly well oiled. He went back at about two in the morning banging doors and waking up the whole household, and finally, mistaking his bedroom, fell in a drunken stupor on to the old man's bed. This latter, who had served in the guards under Napoleon III, wasted no time. He got up, adjusted his night-cap, took the individual by the waist and quite simply threw him out of the window into the farm courtyard, on to a pile of manure which was very conveniently lying there. Because of this, the impact was deadened, and the Prussian, remembering nothing, woke up only in the early hours of the following morning when the hens came to scratch about for food there."

Today there are ten people registering harvest returns in Saint-Cyr-les-Colons-Préhy. Two of them also make a quantity of *Premier Cru*. Approximately half of the production of AOC Chablis is made at the *cave coopérative*. Jean-Marc Brocard is one of the best representatives of the new generation. His wines are superb.

Growers

Brocard, Jean-Marc	86 41 42 11
Légland, Bernard Ardilliers	86 41 42 70
Préhy (GAEC de)	
Reugnis (GAEC des)	86 41 40 44
Sauvageot, Gaston	86 41 42 54
Segard, Michel Les Ouches	86 41 40 53
Seguin, Claude Grande Rue	86 41 42 67

The church at Préhy.

Rameau

Total area of vines under production	Quantity declared as AOC in 1987		
	Chablis 1er Cru	Chablis	Petit-Chablis
4.29 ha	nil	128 hl	36 hl

Rameau is a hamlet in the commune of Collan, which is outside the Chablis region. The vineyards are minute and the quantities produced negligible.

Grower
Dampt, Bernard

Villy

Total area of vines under production	Quantity declared as AOC in 1987		
	Chablis 1er Cru	Chablis	Petit-Chablis
33.56 ha	nil	1 851 hl	164 hl

A very small village between Maligny and Lignorelles, entirely given over to plain AOC Chablis produced by some fifteen growers from vineyards totalling 90 hectares.

Growers			
	Pigé, Pierre		Tupinier, Maurice 86 47 45 95
Bachelier, Raymond 86 47 41 58	Poitout, Daniel 86 47 41 65	Tupinier, Raymond 86 47 42 80
Baillard, Julien	Savary, Olivier Grande Rue 86 47 42 09	
Couturat, Jean 86 47 41 42	Tupinier, Joël	

Viviers

Total area of vines under production	Quantity declared as AOC in 1987		
	Chablis 1er Cru	Chablis	Petit-Chablis
83.10 ha	167 hl	4 792 hl	17 hl

This is the most easterly commune in the Chablis region. The château of Viviers, an elegant seventeenth-century building, stands at the bottom of the village near the springs which were the reason for the first settlement here. The vineyard can claim a long history, for it goes back to the Renaissance. The parcel attached to the château covers about

Viviers is a perfect example of a small viticultural commune in Chablis.

15 hectares. The vines and cellar belong to the dependable firm of Albert Bichot in Beaune. The largest vineyard is that of Jean-Jacques Moreau: it extends over 50 hectares, an unusual phenomenon for the region.

Growers		Gravière (GAEC)	Moreau, Jean-Jacques
			Domaines de Viviers 86 75 92 93
Charlot, Jean	86 75 92 73	Château de Viviers	
		Maison Lupé-Cholet,	
Grandjean, Gérard	86 75 91 72	21700 Nuits-Saint-Georges	

Other communes

Growers	Laroche, Patrick
	Vezannes, 89700 Tonnerre
Albar, Léon	registering in Maligny
Venoy, 89290 Champs-sur-Yonne	
registering in Beine	**Michaut, Jean-Claude**
	Epineuil, 89700 Tonnerre
Gaumont, Jean-Claude	registering in Chichée
Quenne, 89290 Champs-sur-Yonne	
registering in Beine	

80% of Lichine's Chablis goes to the United States.

La Chablisienne

This *coopérative*, the only one in the area, is responsible for approximately a quarter of the production of the Chablis vineyards. Today there are about two hundred members, whose estates vary in size from just a few square yards to 20 hectares. The average works out at three hectares.

La Chablisienne was founded in 1923, at a time when Chablis was in a state of crisis. In the first part of the book, I have related the part played in this story by the priest, Balitran, and his acolytes, Pinsot and Persenoud. After several epic struggles, La Chablisienne really got off the ground in 1947 with the arrival of Monsieur Fortin. He had a vat-house installed for vinification, modern for the period; but because the producers retain the habit of bringing their harvest already in the form of must, the *coopérative* still has no press. Storage capacity is in the order of 60,000 hectolitres.

Once a grower has become a member of La Chablisienne it is not easy for him to withdraw. Otherwise, growers might want their independence during good periods, falling back on the idea of working together with other growers in times of adversity. The quality of each harvest is judged by the executive board, and members are awarded prizes for their contribution, with a possible cash payment for high quality. Jean-Michel Tucki, the present manager, says that his *cave* is "absolutely trustworthy", an observation which we are pleased to endorse. It is entirely representative of the Chablis appellation, for it incorporates the production of some twenty communes in the area.

The total area of the *coopérative* vineyards is around 500 hectares. All the *Grands Crus*, except Valmur, are represented. Among the *Premiers Crus*, Fourchaume is the largest. Wine drinkers may sometimes be under the impression that such and such a wine, with the label of such and such a local grower, is his genuine, individual product. Sometimes it is no such thing, for that particular Chablis may have come from the huge collective vat. But the wine within will at least be consistent. Most of the annual production is marketed in bulk. La Chablisienne supplies wines to the local *négociants*, to the principal firms in Beaune, and to a number of foreign importers.

Globally, La Chablisienne is viewed as a *cave* with an eye to quality. During recent years, it has made considerable investments. It should also be acknowledged that the *coopérative* plays an important role in regulating the market.

Members

Beine
Albar, Léon
Blanvillain, Jacques
Chambre d'agriculture
Lefort, Rémy
Michaut, F (GAEC)
Patrice, Gérard
Robin, Georgette
Roblot, Roger
Villain, Robert

Béru
Bocquet, Henri
Laventureux, Olympe
Pagnier, André

Chablis
Beaux, Félix
Bègue, Jean
Château Grenouille
Condoris, Madeleine
Fèvre, Robert

Gremet, Jean-Marie
Raimond, André
Robin, Henri
Robin, Marie-Claire
Robin, Michel
Simon, Jules
Soupé, Jean-Claude

Chemilly-sur-Serein
Cherbuy, Christian
Detolle, Georges
Detolle, Henri (Mme.)
Detolle, Maurice
Durand, Albert
Faucillon, Raymond
Kaczmar, Edmond
Lavaud, Bernard
Lavaud, Thierry
Lompré, Daniel
Martin, Paul
Mathieu, Roger
Nicolle, Edmond
Patis (GAEC du)
Race, Christian
Race, Jacques

Chichée
Gasser, Jean
Michaut, Eric
Michaut, Michel
Michaut, René
Robin, André (Mme.)
Robin, Jean

Courgis
Adine, Daniel (Mme.)
Adine, Marc (Mme.)
Adine, Maurice
Barbier, Claude
Barbier, Pierre (Mme.)
Bernard, Marie-Louise
Bouc, Gabriel
Bouc, Jacques
Cathelin, Bernard
Chapotin, Jean-Pierre
Chapotin, Philibert
Château (GAEC du)
Ducastelle, Alfred (Mme.)
Dufour, Jean-Robert
Dufour, Robert
Dupré, André
Dupré, Gilbert
Foulley, Jacques
Foulley, Philippe
George, Michel
Jacque, Odette
Landais, Roger
Maingonnat, Raymond (Mme.)
Mineur (Heirs)
Quittot, Françoise
Quittot, Gilbert
Race, André
Race, Gaston (Mme.)
Race, Gilbert
Race, Marcel
Race, Roland
Rétif, Daniel
Rétif, Pierre
Valluet, Yves
Vitteaux, René

Fleys
Barrault, Henri
Chamon, Louis
Collon, Guy
Couperot, Alain
Couperot, Eugène
Couperot, Jean-Louis
Couperot, Roger
Dauvissat, Lionel
Fournillon, Bernard
Gautherin, Robert

Rousseau, Robert
Vaillier, Carmen

Fontenay-près-Chablis
Brousseau, Philippe
Carré, Frères
De Oliveira, Bernard
De Oliveira, P. (GAEC)
Dorey, Henri
Dupas, Guy
Dupas, Henri
Fèvre Frères (GAEC)
Lecestre, André
Lecestre, Jean-Marc
Mathieu, Georges
Mothe, Jean
Moreau, Charles
Porcheron, Ulysse
Rousseau, Jean-Pierre
Rousseau, Pierre
Ventura, Antoine
Ventura, José
Vrignaud, Michel

Fyé
Bonnet, Jean-Marie
Bonnet, Marcel
Bonnet, Maurice (Mme.)
Carré, Pierre
Chapuis, Antoine
Dampt, Bernard
Dauvissat, Michel
Fèvre, Régis
Fèvre, René
Goutant, Charles
Lanier, André
Raoult, Eliane
Rapet, Charles
Renaud, André
SAFER de Bourgogne
Vuillaume, Jean

La Chapelle-Vaupelteigne
Alexandre, Guy
Alignon, Guy
Crochot, Alain
Crochot, Armand
Defert, René
Foynat, Denise
Foynat, Pierre
Jolly, René
Lhoste, André (Mme.)
Lhoste, Jean-Claude
Lhoste, Maurice
Pauley, Pierre
Ratel, Annick
Thouverey, Patrick
Tremblay, Annette
Tremblay, Henri
Tupinier, Marcel

Lignerolles
Beaufumé, Henri
Crochot, Henri
Fassier, Christiane
Gallois, Christiane
Gallois, Marcellin
Pautre, Francis
Pautre, P. and F. (GAEC)
Perrot, Evelyne
Tremblay, Jean-Claude
Tremblay, Suzanne

Maligny
Gautheron, Jacques
Gautheron, Maurice
Jolly, Paul (Mme.)
Jossot, Paul
Jossot, Pierre (Mme.)
Laroche, Patrick
Laroche, Paul
Lorot, Louis

La Chablisienne.

Milly
Bourcey, Jean
Bourcey, Roland
Jannet, Jacques
Jannet, Jean
Mignard, Marcel
Peigne, Fernand
Peigne, Robert
Perrot, Daniel
Villetard, Pierre
Villetard, Raoul

Poilly-sur-Serein
Malaquin, Claude
Moreau, Jacques
Moreau, Pascal

Poinchy
Cottenot, Marcel
Crochot, Georges
Duchemin, Charles
Duchemin, Michel
Jannet, Jacqueline
Mothère, Félix (Mme.)
Roblot, Cécilien (Mme.)
Simonot, Louis
Simonot, Rémy

Préhy
Préhy (GAEC de)
Reugnis (GAEC des)

Serrigny
Fouinat, Roland

Villy
Bachelier, Raymond
Bachelier, Roger
Couturat, Jean
Lecuiller, Gaston (Mme.)
Pige, Pierre
Poitout, Daniel
Sodoyer, Philippe

Viviers
Balacey, Jean
Balacey, Jean-Luc
Charlot, Jean
Grandjean, Gérard
Picq, Bernard

179

The Négociants of Chablis

A handful of Chablis firms represent local business. But many other firms outside the immediate vicinity are keen to offer their clients Chablis wines too. My object here is not to draw up an exhaustive list of all the addresses where Chablis can be bought. I will make only three exceptions in including firms which are outside the area. The first two are Bichot and Drouhin in Beaune which, alphabetically, are near the head of the list which follows. The third is the firm of Nicolas which for three generations has offered its faithful customers great, average and little Chablis wines, carefully selected. As I have often tasted them, I can say that Nicolas's Chablis wines are in the main very acceptable and offer good value for money.

To discover a wine direct from an estate is always exciting. It adds to the pleasure to be able to say: "Just taste this! I found this one myself". But no individual buyer, on the other hand , can claim the experience and ability to choose of a professional. And the *négociants* more often than not have the technical resources to ensure that the wines are delivered in perfect condition.

Increasingly, Chablis wines are being despatched in the bottle.

Berthier, Jean-Claude
2 rue Champ-du-Fort, 89800 Chablis. Tel: 86 42 12 52

Jean-Claude Berthier and his wife take a sort of coquettish delight in claiming that they are "a small firm". They have a few parcels of vines in the Chablis AOC and in Vaillons, and followed their grandfather Jules Heurley into their present business, acting mainly as brokers to firms of *négociants* in Beaune and Mâcon. But they also take care to make sure they are in a position to offer more limited quantities to people wanting to buy as little as one or two cases from the region at the most advantageous price. With Jean-Claude Berthier and his wife there is no place for window-dressing. Sincerity serves to cement their commercial relations. They are therefore entirely dependable.

Bichot, Albert
6 bis bd Jacques Copeau, B.P. 49, 21202 Beaune Cedex. Tel: 80 22 17 99.

About a generation ago, the heirs of Dr Long-Depaquit formed an association with the Bichot family. The firm of "Domaine Long-Depaquit" was born of this union. For nearly ten years Gérard Vullien, from Savoie, has managed the whole of their Chablis vineyards, spread out over the *Grands* and *Premiers Crus* and in the good growing areas of AOC Chablis, Viviers and Béru. The total covers some 40 hectares, of which 9 are in *Grands Crus*. The jewel in the crown is undoubtedly the *cru* of La Moutonne. This *climat* of nearly 2.4 hectares lies where the valley of Vaudésir opens out. Its international reputation is not in proportion to its diminutive size. It is the very quintessence of great Chablis wine and one of the rarest of France's white wines.

The esteemed firm of Bichot exerts a strong influence on its sister-firm, Lupé-Cholet, in Nuits-Saint-Georges. Because it makes good sense economically and administratively, the firm runs the estate of Château de Viviers in Chablis, that is approximately 12 hectares of good vines, with an independent vat-house next to the château itself. Because of this, it can be said that Bichot and its associate are the largest vineyard proprietors "outside Chablis" in the Chablis region. It always amuses me to see that the coat of arms of the Long-Depaquits is flanked by two magnificent greyhounds, whereas that of the Bichots carries the head of a two-antlered stag. The conservationists will be pleased: on this occasion the stag has got the better of the hounds.

Drouhin, Joseph
7 rue d'Enfer, 21200 Beaune

The fingers of two hands are not enough to number the Burgundy *climats* where Drouhin prevails, like the fairy-tale wealth of marquis de Carabas. In Chablis, this *négociant* can walk you round some 30 hectares of vineyards, which includes a 17% participation in La Moutonne in association with Bichot. The whole of the firm's production – Les Clos, Vaudésir, Preuses and several *Premiers Crus* – is aged and bottled in Beaune. The Drouhin style tends towards delicacy, and the distinguished signature, even printed on the label, seems to be able to command the price of a rare autograph.

Fèvre, William
Dne de La Maladière, 14 rue Jules Rathier, 89800 Chablis.
Tel: 86 42 12 51.

We have already met this illustrious Chablisien as a grower. However, it should be mentioned that about 10% of his turnover figure is generated through acting as a *négociant* for AOC Chablis. All the rest stems from the firm's own vineyards. William Fèvre exports 90% of his production, his principal markets being the United States of America, Great Britain and Japan.

Lamblin & Fils
Maligny, 89800 Chablis. Tel: 86 47 40 85

It would be difficult to find a firm more family-minded than this. The chairman, Jacques Lamblin, succeeded his father, and he is assisted by his wife, Ida. Their two sons work alongside them: Michel is the managing director, assisted by his wife, Françoise, and Didier is the technical director, having pursued serious, in-depth studies in oenology. This firm, both producer and *négociant*, is the only one in the Chablis region which is not in the commune of Chablis itself. Twenty-one people are employed full-time, some in the cellars, some in the offices. Commercial activity centres on the export market and accounts for 70% of the turnover, most of it going to EC countries.

The Lamblin family has been working the land here since 1690. They are to be found in Beine, Chablis, Poinchy and Maligny, and are also proprietors in Fourchaume (on the L'Homme Mort side) and in Mont-de-Milieu. As for the other wines they market, they mainly buy in must which they vinify themselves. They age wines partly in wood. Apart from Chablis, they have been marketing a good white table-wine for some years now, a happy diversification. All are to be highly recommended.

Laroche, Henri
12 rue Auxerroise, B.P. 33. 89800 Chablis. Tel: 86 42 14 30.

Michel Laroche, the son of Henri, is descended from a distinguished line of viticulturalists. The founder, Jean-Victor Laroche, was a simple vigneron in Maligny in the middle of the last century. The two most recent generations have made giant strides, creating a little viticultural empire. In the *Grands Crus*, they are to be found at Les Clos, Bougros and Blanchot where, with a certain pride, they cultivate very old vines. They are also to be seen in Fourchaume, Montmains, Vaillons and Beauroy. There have been mergers with the Domaine de la Jouchère and the firm of Josselin Bacheroy.

Laroche is at once an innovatory and a traditionalist firm. It does not hesitate to make audacious, and often judicious, experiments in oenology; now and again, it makes a pilgrimage into the past to rediscover, for example, the benefits of ageing in wood. All this combines to make Laroche a dynamic and dependable firm, with good business sense and motivated by a concern for high quality. One of the recent creations of the firm is the fifty centilitre bottle. This I applaud (keeping one hand free to raise my glass to the sucess of this initiative), for I am convinced of the practicality of this size. On the other hand, I have reservations about the diversification of labels, which can only create confusion in the mind of the wine-lover: Fernand Bacheroy, Jean Baulat, Alain Combard, Paul Dupressoir, Roland Foucard, Henri Josset, Jacques Millar... all these wines flow from the Laroche tap. This doubtless pleases the printers. But, equally, buyers are sure to be perplexed. Whatever the case, the Laroche cellars amass prizes (diplomas, medals, etc.) and they are well run on the commercial level. There is good value for your money to be found here.

J. Moreau & Fils
Route d'Auxerre, 89800 Chablis. Tel: 86 42 40 70

With a storage capacity of 60,000 hectolitres and more than 70 hectares in production, this family business is the largest in the Chablis region. Its story began in 1814 with the arrival of Jean-Joseph Moreau, a cooper by profession, from Dijon. His activities as a wine-merchant grafted themselves quite naturally on to wine production towards the end of the last century. One of the jewels of the family inheritance is the estate of Les Clos des Hospices, which is in Les Clos, in *Grand Cru* Chablis, and is what La Moutonne is to Vaudésir. This was the estate reserved for the Hôpital de Chablis before the Revolution. Its wine is extraordinarily rich in bouquet, powerful and yet delicate. The Moreaus count some 20 hectares in the very best vineyards of the area, and particularly in Vaillons, which is the firm's standard-bearer.

Jean-Jacques Moreau has an excellent palate. His temperament, both modern and critical, means that he takes a keen interest in oenological techniques and passes strict judgement on their results. Certain tedious – some might say jealous – souls do not shrink from pointing an accusing finger at the wines he labels simply "Moreau Blanc", without any other mention of their origin. Personally, I have a great deal of respect for this attitude, for it is indicative of the rigid and extremely high standards of quality the firm sets itself. Moreau is allergic to wood, be it old or new. All his wines have a fresh, clean style which is very "up-to-the-minute".

Moreau reigns supreme over the export markets which constitute the bulk of the firm's turnover. He thinks that the recent extension of the vineyards (especially in the north-west) and the excessively rapid inflation of prices will, sooner or later, prove harmful to the economy of the region. The risk does undoubtedly exist. We shall see. Talleyrand used to say that the only way to overcome difficulties is to sit them out. The firm of Moreau is certainly built to last.

A. Regnard & Fils
Vincensini-Regnard Successeurs, 28 bd Tacussel, 89800 Chablis. Tel: 86 42 10 45

Zéphyr Regnard founded this company in 1860. He was a forebear of the wife of Michel Rémon, who today presides over the firm's fortunes. In 1957, Regnard absorbed the firm of Pic and the two names continue to be managed side by side with different commercial outlets. The principal characteristic of Regnard is its ferocious attachment to Chablis wines which are practically all it sells, which is even more laudable because this firm owns no vines. But Michel Rémon remains close to the land, for he allows no one to take over his personal responsibility for vinification. His methods are rather traditional, despite a certain reticence as regards new wood. The wines are, however, allowed to age for a reasonable period before being bottled. The result is a wide range of thoroughly classical Chablis which preserve a deserved reputation both for the wines themselves and for their vintner. Regnard and Pic and their wines can be entirely depended upon.

Simonnet-Febvre & Fils
9 avenue d'Oberwesel, 89800 Chablis. Tel: 86 42 11 73.

Jean-Claude Simonnet was born to wear the robes of the Piliers Chablisiens, so much so that at official functions it is rare to see him in an ordinary suit. He is in his element when ritual and corporate dignity are the order of the day, though this is in no way to deny his sparkling wit. Speaking of "sparkling", the firm of Simonnet-Febvre makes some quite delicious Champagne method *crémants* de Bourgogne. As far as I know, they are the only ones from Chablis which offer competition to the dream-merchants of Reims and Epernay. The sparkling wines of Simonnet-Febvre frolic and gambol on your lips, a dance in the very best of taste. They are extremely good in their own right, and no mere imitations of Champagne, though many years ago Jean-Claude Simonnet's great-grandfather was employed by a certain M. Tisserand, who used to sell his sparkling wines under the name of Moët et Chandon. Today there is no dissembling as to the nature of the products coming from the firm of Simonnet.

Apart from these sublime productions, the firm of Simonnet-Febvre has a large range of the best Chablis *crus*, in particular Montée de Tonnerre, Mont de Milieu, Fourchaume and Vaillons, the jewel being the firm's Preuses. You can also find good little wines from Irancy or other vineyards round about. Even if Jean-Claude makes you smile, it cannot be denied that his firm is a serious one.

Appendices

Vintage chart for Chablis

Marks out of 20 for the last twenty-seven vintages							
1989	18	1979	14	1969	17
1988	17	1978	18	1968	5
1987	15	1977	10	1967	14
1986	17	1976	17	1966	15
1985	17	1975	18	1965	3
1984	12	1974	9	1964	14
1983	15	1973	15	1963	8
1982	16	1972	6	1962	16
1981	17	1971	16	1961	18
1980	12	1970	16		

An anthology of poetry from Chablis

THE VIGNERON'S WEEK

On Monday, I 'as a drop to drink
To try to drown my cares;
I goes and sits and 'as a think
I works as slowly as I dares.
The boss, no 'eart 'e's got
When t'lads is runnin' short.
When I puts away me tot
He glowers, the damn spoilsport.
He glowers, the damn spoilsport.

On Tuesday, I 'as to shift some soil.
(Some fellers 'elp me, mind)
Th'boss, 'e loves to snaipe us toil;
'E's never slow to find
Some job that takes all day.
'E stands there lookin' on
And never goes away
Till after t'sun 'as gone.
Till after t'sun 'as gone.

On We'n'sday, I gets a right ol' shock:
I 'ave to make some layers;
But up comes th'boss, a-wearin' 'is smock.
Of course, 'e 'as to show us
The proper way to bind
All t'prunings up together.
'E drives yer out yer mind,
The clever show-off feller.
The clever show-off feller.

On Thursday, I goes down to t'vines
To earth up th'roots, 'gainst frost;
But th'boss is there before – poor swine,
Just stands there lookin' lost.
"Come on", 'e says, "start weedin'!
Th'ground's not too 'ard today."
"I'm worried 'bout th'vines freezin',
But 'av it thee own way.
But 'av it thee own way."

'On Friday, it's same ol' tale again,
I'm off to do some plantin';
I takes along o'me some men
An' all is goin' smashin'
When th'boss brings us some wine
(Arr, very trimly bottled)
But what a drop, the swine!
Nay chance o' gettin' sozzled.
Nay chance o' gettin' sozzled.

On Sat'day th'week comes to a close.
I'm off to do some hoein'.
Th'boss sticks in his damn great nose
To find out where we're goin'.
"I don't want thee to hoe
When t'crops is in good shape;
It's just a dodge, I know,
To eat up all t'best grapes.
To eat up all t'best grapes."

On Sunday, they dance in t'village 'all;
I goes along to watch 'em.
"Come on you lot, it's great!", they call;
But not to me, God rot 'em!
I'm miserable as sin.
To every lass and lad
I'm nowt but a bumpkin.
It makes me 'oppin' mad.
It makes me 'oppin' mad.

SONNET TO CHABLIS

Our region's filled with many a famous site:
Buildings and monuments you scarce can list;
To praise them all, the poet needs to write
Hundreds of sonnets, if none is to be missed.

The River Yonne, in order alphabetic
Is, it is true, right at the very last;
But through its splendid role in matters Bacchic
Comes first of all, the rest clearly surpassed.

Deck'd with a priceless jewel, pure and fair,
Its name well known, its character most rare,
Paris itself cannot produce its peer.

Bright in my glass it sparkles and it gleams,
Laughing and merry, nectar of our dreams.
Chablis, divine, unique, we thee revere.

Fernand Clas

186

CHABLIS

Around this jocund board I see
Good friends: a serried host.
Of favour fair, full readily
Each doth his fellow toast.
And when in each man's glass, serene,
The sparkling wine shines clear,
There mirrored is in every mien
An unaffected cheer.

Refrain
Chablis, Chablis,
Strong vines, far-famed in verse.
From Les Beugnons right to the Preuses
There is but fair Chablis!

The joyous vines in verdant glee
Rise proudly up the slopes.
The vintner smiles at wine-to-be
'Twill fill his casks, he hopes.
And wine of Moutonne or Les Clos,
In flask or barrel found,
Will ever see its fame to grow,
Its quality renowned.

Refrain

Be it our care and hope to store
Our weal – so highly prized,
Of our fair France that gem so pure,
A wealth our sires devised.
Behold the vines with fruit bedecked;
'Tis by our toil thereto.
Let's worthy be of that respect
Which is the worker's due.

Refrain

Chablis, thy name we must defend,
Abused by foreign foes.
Thy Bacchic lore we will extend
Until the whole world knows.
Hard though the struggle prove to be,
We ne'er shall be downcast,
For we respect our liberty,
In brotherhood bound fast.

Félix Beau
A veteran Chablis vigneron.

CHABLIS

When you feel yourself downcast,
Far from Paris you must flee,
And to cheer yourself at last
Turn your steps towards Chablis.
Your appetite will be renewed
So make your way to the restaurant
Owned by Monsieur Bergerand,
Where gourmets can enjoy good food.

Refrain

Chablis, Chablis,
O land I love.
Hail evermore to thee
Great gift from Heaven above!
Chablis, Chablis,
Magic town,
From care you set us free.

Drink and shut the world away.
And if the steep slope finds you pained
By too much weight in disarray,
Your legs and lungs are overstrained
By mighty Vaux-Flot on your way,
Your magic bottle take from store:
Wine will bring the spirit glee
And make you light as any bee.

Refrain

Friend, who wander in these vines,
Do not fear the grape's good juice;
The ecstasy it brings us is divine,
Careless content it will induce.
Blithe and, as the birds are, free,
Let us raise our happy song.
Let the chorus echo long:
Hail to the splendid ninety-three!

Refrain

On coats of arms of Chablis town
Why does no cross of fame appear?
Your sons have brought you great renown
In war, and cost you many a tear.
In times of peace your good vines' fruit
Fills men with vigour and romance;
Sun-tanned and strong, without dispute,
They'll soon beget more sons for France.

Refrain

Aristide Bruand, 1895

With fine fresh oysters for my fare,
Good Chablis wine is pure delight!
Both fame and fortune I'd forswear
To succumb to this wine so bright
With fine fresh oysters for my fare!
(De Courcy)

Jean Pinard,
Canon Trottier, eighteenth century

Wine of Nevers and Sancerre,
Wine of Verdelai, of Auxerre,
Of Tonnerre and Flavigny,
Saint-Porchain and Savigny,
Wine of Chablis and of Beaune,
As pale a yellow as moonstone,
Greener is than horn of ram,
But other wines care not a damn;
Such wines as these are a blessing;
Serve them all before the king...

Henri d'Andely,
La Bataille des Vins, 1214

A friar from Auxerre
On Twelfth Night, I declare,
At Mass was not on cue,
A-snoring in his pew.
A cantor came to say:
"Now when they start to pray
It's your turn to intone
The seventh antiphon."
Thus roused, in great alarm,
He clean forgot the psalm
And cried: "Bring wine from blest Tonnerre
To help me chant the prayer!"

Colle, eighteenth century

In a well-ordered house:

Wine of Auxerre and Burgundy,
Wine of Beaune and Gascony,
Wine of Chablis and of Givry,
Wine of Vertus and Irancy.

Eustache Deschamps,
known as Morel,
Bailiff of Senlis and Treasurer
of France, 1340

Chablis
You capture me,
Enrapture me.
So be!

Your wine
Lulls me,
Dulls me,
Divine!

Carefree
You charm me
You calm me.
Chablis.

Anonymous, sixteenth century

My wine is strong and when you have drunk, it envelops you,
enchants the palate and leaves a suave flavour of mushrooms.

Canon Gaudin,
Letter to Madame d'Epinay, c. 1765

'Twas in the verdant spring, this glorious leap-year
Your cherished virtue I defiled:
Unblemished pages white, where soon each fine idea
Of gourmets is to be compiled.

But is it right that I, who count of years three-score
To point the road should now begin,
That path which you must take, hard by Cythera's shore,
Which leads to Brillat-Savarin?

Come forward, my good lords, make haste, each with his Dame,
And visit now our Chablis fair.
The hotel Bergerand false splendour doth disclaim;
For all awaits a welcome rare.

'Tis time, dear friends, to go, for I must quit the stage.
I'm chastened when I think with gloom
That my reward will be, when you reach the last page
To be pushing up the daisies' bloom!

L. Long Depaquit
May 1952

What a fine priest we have, my dear,
To cure our souls round here.
Let Chambertin or pure Chablis
Fill oft his proffered glass;
For he takes away our sins, you see,
If we attend his mass.

   Debailleul, to the Alcazar
       c. 1910

Ne'er fades from memory's span
Dry Chablis, bright and clear;
From out whose charms it teaches man
The oyster to revere.

Pierre Antoine Augustin,
Chevalier de Piis, c. 1820

For delicate, refined dishes, we choose the wines of Chablis, Tonnerre and Coulange...

Frédéric Léonard,
L'art de bien traiter,
(The art of good catering), 1674

Dave
You knave:
I now crave
Some good Blanchot.
Quick! Come here a mo
And make my glass o'erflow.
The wines their savour reap
In wood where they steep.
Full many a nip
Makes me sleep.
I'll sip
Deep.

Charles-François Panard, 1694-1765

Index of growers and vineyard managers

191

Picture acknowledgements:
All the photographs in this book are by
Michel Plassart, Nantes
with the exception of those by Alain Geoffroy, Chablis (pages 18, 22 top)